THE AMERICAN CHRISTMAS

THE MACMILLAN COMPANY
NEW YORK · CHICAGO
DALLAS · ATLANTA · SAN FRANCISCO

**THE MACMILLAN COMPANY
OF CANADA, LIMITED**
TORONTO

"THREE KINGS" *by Edmund D. Lewandowski,*
American Third Prize, First Hallmark Art Award

The

AMERICAN CHRISTMAS

A Study in National Culture

by JAMES H. BARNETT

1954 THE MACMILLAN COMPANY · NEW YORK

To Esther and Susan

Foreword and Acknowledgments

This is an interpretative study of the Christmas festival celebrated in contemporary United States. It is directed to the
general educated reader, and seeks to understand rather than
to praise or to criticize the celebration. Though it offers information and explanations of modern holiday customs and
behavior, it does not pretend to advance an inclusive theory
to account for the origin and development of Christmas in this
country. I do not believe that the present state of knowledge
concerning the festival warrants such an attempt at this time.

One reason for this is that there is as yet an inadequate body
of significant, authenticated facts concerning the historical
development of Christmas in the United States from which
such a theory might be derived. Though there is abundant
folklore and anecdotal literature on the American Christmas,
scholarly studies in this field are scarce and a great deal of
historical research will have to be done before the emergence
of the celebration, particularly during the nineteenth century,
can be established beyond question.

On the other hand, it is possible to learn a great deal about
the contemporary celebration through the use of statistical
data, interviews, newspaper and magazine reports, question-

naires, observation and participation in holiday activities. These devices provide information and insights which enable one to grasp the nature of Christmas and some of its connections with American society and culture. I have also drawn on the slight but interesting body of scholarly writings on Christmas which have appeared in recent years. In addition, holiday art, music, and literature have been studied in the effort to learn how these cultural elements preserve the traditional meanings and forms of Christmas, yet also reflect the impact of modern life on the festival.

From the above, it appears that an indigenous, national Christmas developed in this country during the nineteenth century which differed from prior celebrations in the British Isles and in several European nations. It crystallized in most parts of the United States by 1860 and altered little in essentials after that time. Commercial influences entered the festival during the latter part of the last century, but made their strongest impact on it after 1920. Secular aspects of the celebration now rival the Christian observances of the occasion, and would probably persist even if its religious significance should diminish. It is also clear that the bonds of family, brotherhood, and even nationalism have become intertwined with the symbolism of the celebration, and few persons are immune to such a combination of influences. For this reason Christmas makes a powerful impact on most Americans, as evidenced either by their efforts to celebrate it in the conventional manner or by their attempts to deny its claims.

The organization of materials by chapters, the emphases, and so on, have been dictated by convenience rather than by any research design or theoretical considerations because this study has been conceived and executed chiefly at a descriptive level. I have tried to combine the viewpoint of social history with that of sociological analysis, and have ventured occasional interpretations derived from psychodynamic psychology. Although this eclectic approach has the defects of its virtues, Christmas is sufficiently complex to warrant study from several different perspectives. Therefore I have consciously adopted whatever approaches seemed most likely to illuminate the character of the empirical materials rather than to confine myself to the precepts of any one discipline.

This book is a pioneer effort in the sociological study of American holidays, and if it stimulates others to a more systematic type of research in this field I will have achieved one of my objectives in undertaking the present volume. Beyond this, it is my sincere hope that those who read this discussion of the national Christmas will gain some new understanding both of the festival and of American culture.

While engaged in writing this book, I have been most fortunate in securing generous assistance from a number of persons and agencies. These are too numerous to mention in all instances, but the following were particularly helpful: Miss Virginia Knox, Law Librarian, and Miss Doris Cook, Newspaper Librarian, at the Connecticut State Library, and Miss Roberta Smith, Reference Librarian at the Wilbur Cross Library of the University of Connecticut. My thanks are also due the library staff of the American Jewish Committee and of the New-York Historical Society. Though I lack his present address, I gratefully acknowledge the assistance of Mr. John Schelander, erstwhile graduate student at the University of Connecticut, for examining certain newspaper files on Christmas.

My thanks are hereby expressed to Dr. Leslie Dent Johnston for drawing my attention to several important scholarly works on Christmas and the cult of St. Nicholas, and for the loan of his valuable doctoral thesis "Classical Origins of Christmas Customs" (1936). I am also greatly indebted to Professor and Mrs. Walter Landauer for translating into English some important Dutch materials on St. Nicholas, and to Mr. Sidney Croog for translating passages on Christmas from an authoritative work published in Danish. Mr. Frank Wei-

tenkampf, formerly curator of prints at the New York
Public Library, provided invaluable information about early
American pictures of Santa Claus and guided me to some of
the first drawings of this figure. Dr. Marvin Sussman gen-
erously sent me a copy of certain parts of his doctoral thesis
which were relevant to Christmas observances. Mr. John H.
Hatcher, Jr., kindly let me have a copy of the opinion *Ex
parte Santa Claus* issued by his father, Judge John H.
Hatcher, in 1927. Mr. Robert L. May, both through corre-
spondence and a personal interview, furnished interesting and
useful information concerning the career of Rudolph the
Red-Nosed Reindeer. In addition, Johnny Marks, who wrote
the song about Rudolph, gave me an enlightening account of
its creation. Likewise, I record my appreciation for the information furnished by Valentine Davies concerning the
writing of *Miracle on 34th Street.*

My thanks are hereby expressed to Mr. Charles Barnett,
Mr. Stanley Lorenson, and to Professors George Simpson,
Solon Kimball, and Harold S. Jacoby for assistance in distributing questionnaires on gift exchanging at Christmas.
Walter H. Baker Company and Samuel French, Inc., gen-
erously permitted me to examine a large number of Christmas
plays at my leisure. Stanley Burnshaw gave me helpful counsel on matters of English style and clarity of expression.

At the University of Connecticut, both colleagues and the
university administration were helpful in many ways. A
sabbatic leave for the first semester of the academic year
1951–1952 made it possible to do a major part of the writing,
and a reduced teaching load after that time enabled me to
complete it. I am particularly indebted to Provost Albert E.
Waugh, who early displayed an interest in this book and
steadily encouraged me in the study of our national holidays.
A number of colleagues gave me valuable assistance and provided useful criticism and counsel. Among these, I am especially grateful to Walter I. Wardwell and Philip E. Taylor.

The indefatigable Charles Niles, News Coordinator at the university, will be surprised to learn that the amount of popular interest aroused by our joint story on Rudolph in December, 1950, helped me decide to write this book.

Finally, I take the greatest pleasure in acknowledging the assistance of my wife, Esther Dodge Barnett. She has helped me understand Christmas, has done extensive typing on the manuscript at all stages of its development, and has maintained those conditions of domestic tranquillity so auspicious for writing.

JAMES H. BARNETT

UNIVERSITY OF CONNECTICUT
STORRS, CONNECTICUT

Table of Contents

Table of Contents

THE AMERICAN CHRISTMAS

CHAPTER I

Christmas in the Making

A distinctive national Christmas developed in the United States during the nineteenth century. Its traditional elements came from English and European sources, but in the new setting these were altered by powerful currents of an emerging American civilization. Like other popular celebrations, Christmas drew vitality both from Christian and from pagan sources. It was anchored in the biblical account of the Nativity, but also contained European folk beliefs and practices which revealed Greek, Roman, and Teutonic influences.

Early colonists brought both religious and folk features of the celebration with them and contributed the cultural base on which the national festival developed. In addition, during the middle decades of the last century, the figure of Santa Claus appeared and began to dominate its folk aspects. About the same time, the Christmas writings of Charles Dickens reemphasized the importance of Christian charity and encouraged the nascent humanitarianism of the period. All these factors affected the development of our national Christmas in very important ways.

Scholars have paid little attention to the history and character of the American Christmas, though the European celebration has been studied carefully.[1] Except for fragmentary descriptions of the holiday customs of parochial groups, the only substantial work on the national celebration is Richards's *How Christmas Came to the Sunday-Schools.* The secular aspects of the festival have received no systematic treatment. This is due, in part, to the paucity of written materials on the festival. In the main, knowledge of Christmas folk beliefs and customs has been preserved and transmitted by the spoken word.

In spite of limitations of historical evidence, it is possible to trace the general origins and development of the national Christmas. Since its religious observance was the source of bitter denominational quarrels during the seventeenth and eighteenth centuries, this conflict provides a pertinent approach to the topic.

The Churches and Christmas

Few Americans are aware that large groups of colonists objected to Christmas during the seventeenth and eighteenth centuries. Many loathed it as an "abomination" even though others observed the occasion as a religious feast. In general, Puritans, Baptists, Presbyterians, and Quakers strongly opposed the religious observance of Christmas, but members of the Church of England, the Dutch Reformed, Lutheran, and Roman Catholic churches, as well as the German sects, carefully followed their traditional celebrations. Religious, ethnic, and national ties were intermixed in defining attitudes toward the festival.

Christmas came to the American colonies while it was the subject of strenuous controversy in England. For the Church of England, the Feast of the Nativity was one of the most important of the year, even though the English Puritans condemned it as "popish" and the secular celebration as a "wonton Bacchanalian feast." New England Puritans shared this hostile attitude toward observing Christmas. Early records indicate that on December 25, 1620, they worked at the erection of their first building in what has been called a "studied neglect" of the day.[2]

Opposition of the English Puritans to festivals culminated in an act of Parliament in 1647 which abolished the observance of Christmas, Easter, and Whitsuntide. This was echoed in 1659 when Puritans of the American colonies enacted a law in the General Court of Massachusetts to punish those who "kept Christmas":

. . . anybody who is found observing, by abstinence from labor, feasting, or any other way, any such days as Christmas day, shall pay for every such offense five shillings.[3]

As early as 1621, Governor Bradford of the Plymouth Colony publicly reprimanded several "lusty younge men" of the colony who maintained that it was against their conscience to work on Christmas day but were discovered at play on the streets on this day. According to Bradford, ". . . some were pitching ye barr, and some playing at stoole-ball and such like sports." [4]

Immigration brought additional members of the Church of England to the Plymouth, Salem, and Boston communities. This was accompanied by schismatic movements among the New England Puritans, and led to a gradual lessening of severity of laws governing the observance of religious festivals. The year 1681 saw the law against the celebration of Christmas repealed, but many of the Puritans were not reconciled to this action. In 1685 Judge Sewell, a Puritan, wrote concerning Christmas:

Some, somehow observe the day, but are vexed, I believe, that the Body of the People Profane it; and, blessed be God, no Authority yet to compel them to keep it.[5]

The judge was pleased that the shops were open and carts rolling into town on Christmas day.

One of the Puritan doctrinal objections to Christmas was the belief that Church government should not ordain anything contrary to, or not found in, the Scriptures. Because the Bible did not prescribe special religious feasts, therefore:

. . . the strict Puritan discarded as "devices of men" all feasts except the Sabbath, the liturgy with its required prayers and Scripture readings and the use of vestments and ornaments.[6]

This view excluded the religious observance of Christmas. However, the English Puritans accepted the historic character of the Nativity.

It should be added that secular reveling at Christmas in England had often interfered with religious devotions and offended the Puritans' moral sense. This intensified their sectarian hostility to the religious observance of Christmas. They brought this attitude with them, and maintained it for the better part of two centuries in parts of New England.

Even though several religious groups opposed Christmas, Episcopalians throughout the colonies observed it as a traditional religious festival. They held morning church services and enjoyed the season with liberal eating, drinking, visiting, and parties. In New York the Dutch settlers observed an extended holiday period which was both religious and secular in nature. Public offices closed during the Christmas season, which began during the early part of December. The Dutch celebrated St. Nicholas (or Sinterklaas) Day on December 6th, but gradual numerical dominance of English settlers shifted the midwinter festival to December 25th. Concerning the difference between the attitude of the Dutch and the Puritans toward Christmas observance, one writer said:

The tranquil, contented burghers . . . were sure to make the most of Christmas-tide and their neighbors who cursed it must have seemed to them the most whimsical of lunatics.[7]

In other colonies attitudes toward Christmas conformed to denominational and ethnic ties of the settlers. Considerable variation in local attitudes and customs was the rule. Communities settled mainly by Roman Catholic, Episcopalian, or Dutch Reformed colonists observed Christmas, while those dominated by Quakers, Baptists, Congregationalists, and Presbyterians vigorously denounced it. This was the pattern of Christmas keeping throughout the seaboard colonies during the period from 1620 to about 1750.

The tendency of the majority of the Puritan settlers to identify the Church of England with royal officials and Toryism in politics added a political factor to their denominational opposition to doctrines and practices of the established church. For this reason celebration of the Nativity by the Church of England drew the fire of Puritan criticism in part because it symbolized the "established order" in a political as well as in an ecclesiastical sense. However, it should be noted that some Puritans in New England celebrated Christmas in spite of ecclesiastical hostility to the festival.[8]

This conflict continued throughout the seventeenth and first half of the eighteenth century, but with diminished intensity. Richards has offered an interesting explanation of the lessened opposition to Christmas observances during the latter part of the eighteenth century. She believes it was due primarily to the increase of immigration from Germanic countries which traditionally celebrated Christmas both as a religious and as a folk occasion.[9] However, it is also true that Scotch-Irish immigration of the eighteenth century brought many who were hostile to the Church of England and, therefore, to Christmas. Consequently the controversy persisted through most of the eighteenth century. Thus religious, political, and perhaps social class differences found expression in disagreement over the ancient celebration.

The latter half of the eighteenth century saw a swing of attention to the realm of economics and politics and religious controversies, including that of Christmas observance, became of less importance, though their causes persisted. The fact that English and Hessian troops celebrated Christmas during the Revolutionary War may have added a patriotic note to the denominational controversy. General Washington crossed the Delaware River on the night of December 25, 1776, to surprise and defeat the Hessian troops stationed at Trenton, New Jersey. In the opinion of one writer, Washington's bold venture succeeded because the Hessians were enjoying their customary Christmas revels and failed to maintain the usual watch and patrols.[10]

Puritan opposition to the festival continued throughout the eighteenth century, but showed decreasing intensity as the nineteenth century opened. Though controversy persisted over the religious celebration, secular interest in the occasion spread rapidly. In 1827 Bishop Chase, an Episcopalian, wrote to his wife: "The devil has stolen from us . . . Christmas, the day of our spiritual redemption and converted it into a day of worldly festivity, shooting and swearing." [11] His words were prophetic of the increasing secularization of Christmas which occurred in the United States during that century. In an indirect way this process was probably influenced by the separation of church and state established by the American Constitution in 1791. Because of this, members of the Puritan and evangelical churches were less inclined to oppose the secular celebration when it no longer symbolized the religious and political dominance of the Church of England. This tolerance increased during the nineteenth century and undoubtedly encouraged popularity of the folk festival.

Sunday schools were established during the first half of the nineteenth century and spread rapidly among Protestant denominations. During this time the religious celebration of Christmas was introduced piecemeal into the Sunday schools, and denominations once opposed to the celebration gradually accepted it. The American Sunday School Union, organized in 1824, undertook to provide lesson materials for use in local church schools. At first it was necessary to avoid controversial issues in the materials, since several denominations clashed on theology. Christmas observance was one of these. Owing to this fact, it received little attention in publications of the union during the decades of 1830–1850, but Richards remarks that:

By 1859 the general attitude towards Christmas had changed sufficiently for the Sunday School Times, starting in that year as a Sunday School Union publication, to contain accounts of Christmas celebrations in individual Sunday Schools and to include in its December numbers Christmas hymns and references to the holiday season.[12]

By about 1870 Christmas was an accepted lesson topic in the publications of the Sunday School Union. This demonstrates a widespread change in the attitude of most denominations toward Christmas between 1830 and 1870. An interesting confirmation of this is found in the fact that many of the popular Christmas songs of a religious character were composed between the years 1850 and 1868.[13]

As the religious celebration appeared in the church school, certain traits of the secular holiday were also introduced. Sunday schools began to integrate these with the religious ones. Thus in 1847 a Sunday-school Christmas tree was set up in a New York City Episcopalian Sunday school.[14] Carols were sung, and gifts were provided for the "underprivileged children." Lesson materials admonished the well favored to share their worldly goods with the less fortunate at Christmas.

As secular customs appeared in the church schools, some were found inappropriate to the religious setting. For example, by 1877 gift giving was being abused because some children apparently went to Sunday school at Christmas only, to obtain a gift. They were called "Christmas Bummers."[15]

Critics began to demand elimination of gifts in the Sunday-school services, and praised the religious duty of Christian charity. Difficulties of this type continue to plague Sunday schools even today.

There were other evidences of growth of the secular folk festival. Advertisements of Christmas gifts were known as early as 1820 [16] in New York City papers and appeared in a Hartford, Connecticut, paper by 1834.[17] The commercial exploitation of Christmas sentiments and customs had begun, and the church was forced to make adjustments to these secular practices.[18]

However, denominational opposition to the ecclesiastic observance of Christmas continued into the second half of the nineteenth century. One can see this in an account of Christmas services in the New York *Daily Times* for December 26, 1855:

The churches of the Presbyterians, Baptists and Methodists were not open on Dec. 25 except where some Mission Schools had a celebration. They do not accept the day as a Holy One, but the Episcopalian, Catholic and German Churches were all open. Inside they were decked with evergreens.

The same account announced the celebration of the Feast of the Nativity and the Midnight Mass at the Roman Catholic Church of the Nativity and at St. Stephen's Church in New York City. However, as the century advanced, traditional opposition to Christmas slowly disappeared, and a church historian has remarked that "by 1880 . . . the religious significance of Christmas had been growing in all evangelical churches." [19] In the twentieth century Sunday schools of the Protestant denominations have embraced Christmas widely both as a religious and as a social celebration. In addition, both Roman Catholic and Protestant churches now commemorate the Nativity by special services, and their members participate in the folk celebration as well, thus reflecting gradual changes in religious thinking and a popular inclination to celebrate both aspects of the occasion.[20]

Folk Beliefs and Customs

Though the Puritans of New England outlawed both the religious observance and social celebration of Christmas for a number of years, many early colonists did not share their anti-Christmas attitudes. Folk festivals persisted even in parts of New England dominated by the Puritans.[21] In the area around New York City, in Pennsylvania, and in the Southern colonies, both religious and folk celebrations were customary in the seventeenth and eighteenth centuries. Most of the Christmas folk customs came to this country from England, Holland, and Germany.

Colonists from these countries emphasized eating, drinking, family gatherings, merrymaking, and joyousness during the Christmas season, which usually began well in advance of December 25th and extended often to January 6th. Food and drink consumed by each group reflected national customs. Usually a holiday salutation was customary in greeting friends, relatives, and even strangers during the season.

The yule-log custom was brought from England, though the island practice of serving the boar's head was not widely adopted. Small whole pigs were used sometimes as a substitute. English colonists contributed mince pies and plum pudding to the Christmas dinner. They also brought the "wassail" custom with them. Though the term originally meant "warm ale," it later embraced a wide variety of special Christmas beverages. A somewhat romanticized account of a family Christmas celebration in "Old Virginia," an area settled by Church of England colonists, described the wassailing as follows:

. . . there is the clink of glasses and cups; the good old vintages, which give nobody a headache, cheer the heart; and the lord of the manor raises his glass and with a smile on his ruddy face, drinks to the general joy of the whole table.[22]

Caroling was a Christmas folk practice which became popular quickly in the colonies and was taken over by many groups. Carols included both religious and folk songs which had grown up about the season. In addition, the English brought their traditional custom of decorating houses and public buildings with holly, ivy, and mistletoe. They emphasized mirth, good fellowship, and the folk quality of Christmas even though many attended religious services and regarded the Nativity as a holy day.

Christmas gifts were not emphasized by the early English colonists, though the wealthy were expected to be generous to the poor. Children received small presents, but they did not think of Christmas primarily as a time when they expected gifts. In common with some of the Pennsylvania German settlers, the English were familiar with the school custom of "Barring the Master" just before Christmas.[23]

The Dutch colonists brought to New Amsterdam (New York) a number of Christmas traits which were incorporated later into the American celebration. Chief among these was the visit of St. Nicholas, who was popular with Catholics and Protestants alike in Holland. He was adopted by many of the American colonists, but lost his ecclesiastical appearance in the process. Dutch lore about St. Nicholas centered on his December 5th visit, when he brought presents to good children and switches for the bad. They were taught to leave some hay for the white horse on which he traveled. Both the Dutch and the Germans gave small gifts to children at Christmas, and stressed the season as of special importance to the young. Like the English settlers, they considered Christmas chiefly a time of merriment and communal joy. It was regarded as a season, not as a day or a brief festival.[24]

In addition to the Christmas customs they shared with the English and New York Dutch, the Germans who settled in Pennsylvania brought the Christmas tree with them. An account of a Christmas celebration held in Bethlehem, Pennsylvania, on December 25, 1747, includes the statement: "For this occasion several small pyramids and one large pyramid of green brushwood had been prepared, all decorated with candles and the large one with apples and pretty verses." [25] This brushwood pyramid was probably the progenitor of the Christmas tree. According to Sowder, Hessian soldiers stationed in the American colonies during the Revolutionary War used Christmas trees to celebrate the holiday.[26] Between the years 1832 and 1851 Christmas trees appeared in Cambridge, Philadelphia, Rochester, Richmond, Wooster, and Cleveland. The custom was fairly common in the United States before it was introduced into England, and owes little or nothing to English practice.

Among the Pennsylvania Germans the name of the Christmas gift bringer was Christkindlein or Kris Kringle. He came on Christmas Eve, December 24th, rather than on December 5th, the Eve of St. Nicholas's Day. They were also familiar with the figure of Belsnickel, known as Knecht Rupprecht in Germany, who was reputed to be the servant of St. Nicholas. He was a threatening figure who punished bad children and rewarded the good with presents.

Pennsylvania German children decorated their trees with animal cookies, apples, strings of popcorn, and brightly colored paper. Some sects, such as the Moravians, put lighted candles on their trees as early as 1752, and later placed them in windows, as became the custom on Beacon Hill in Boston.

The construction of Christmas "yards" or "gardens" was a common practice among the Pennsylvania Germans, but their reproduction of the manger scene, known as the *Putz*, is a more widely known trait.[27] In recent years it has diffused to many sections of the United States. Nativity scenes appear at Christmas in Protestant homes today as well as in those of Roman Catholics and the German sectarian groups.

The beliefs, symbols, and customs described above entered this country between 1620 and 1800. By informal means they spread throughout the settled areas, with resulting community variation. Between the years 1800 and 1860 both the religious and the folk aspects of Christmas diffused widely. Each section of the country developed a Christmas celebration which mirrored its local culture, national backgrounds, and natural surroundings. A few passages will indicate the variety of regional Christmas celebrations.

The modern Southern custom of setting off firecrackers and shooting guns at Christmas is foreshadowed in a passage from the North Carolina *Wilmington Daily Journal* for December 23, 1851:

John Barleycorn retained his usual spirit . . . and our town authorities on Christmas generally let the boys have their way so far as mere noise is concerned. There was therefore much firing of crackers, rockets, sarpients, etc. and a good deal of cheering and shouting, but nothing worse and as the night wore on even these ceased and the town slept.[28]

As settlers pushed west and ethnic groups clustered in localities, their traditional Old World Christmas celebrations appeared. Heilbron wrote in 1849 of a Christmas celebration in Minnesota:

On Christmas morning, "the grave and devout will be at church" . . . Church-going was a natural part of the frontier holiday observance; in fact, it was taken for granted and was seldom the subject of comment. A Swedish-Lutheran pastor . . . complained that he found it necessary to prepare his sermon in a saloon near Shakopee, "where several drunkards made a lot of disturbance until late at night." At Faribault the yule celebration began in the Episcopal Cathedral at six in the morning with a carol service, which by the late seventies was looked upon as "one of the time-honored customs of the parish." [29]

Here the religious and folk aspects of the celebration dwelt side by side with little conflict because the traditional pattern had carried over to the New World.

In Texas, Christmas was celebrated with vigor, as indicated by the following passage written in 1839:

It is now 9 o'clock, P.M. and tomorrow's Christmas. The way the votaries of that jolly god Bacchus are "humping" it is curious. Fiddles groan under a heavy weight of oppression, and heel-taps suffer to the tune of "We Won't Go Home 'Till Morning" and now and then the discharge of firearms at a distance, remind me that merriment now despotic rules to the utter discomfiture of dull care, while I, O Jeminy! have nothing stronger wherewith to lash my cold sluggish blood than water.[30]

This lament strikes a familiar note in several descriptions of the folk observance of Christmas in Texas during the mid-nineteenth century.

A botanist, William H. Brewer, traveled up and down the state of California during the years 1860–1864 and described a Christmas spent in San Francisco in 1862.

I was at church this morning, an Episcopal church, all decorated with evergreens and this afternoon it seemed as if all the city was in the streets. The customs of Europe and the East are transplanted here, churches are decked with evergreens, Christmas trees are the fashion . . . there is no snow visible even on the distant mountains. Christmas here, to me, represents a date, a festival, but not a season.[31]

This passage suggests elements of the later national Christmas by mentioning evergreens in the churches and the popular Christmas tree. The author's regret at the absence of snow and wintry scenes anticipates the contemporary inclination to associate snow, ice, and wintry weather with Christmas.

An editorial passage in *Brother Jonathan* (1842) indicates that Christmas was already regarded as the children's celebration in the New York City area:

Tomorrow will be Christmas, jolly rosy Christmas, the Saturnalia of children. Ah, how the little rogues long for the advent of this day; for with it comes their generous friend Santa Claus with his sleigh, like the purse of Fortunatus, over-flowing with treasures.[32]

Here appear the themes of children, Santa Claus, his sleigh, and untold treasure for the "little rogues." These elements have become central to the contemporary American Christmas.

The "Carol Philosophy" of Dickens

A new element was added to the American Christmas about the middle of the nineteenth century. This was the "carol philosophy" of Charles Dickens, which combined certain religious and secular attitudes toward the celebration into a humanitarian pattern. It excoriated individual selfishness and extolled the virtues of brotherhood, kindness, and generosity at Christmas. For Dickens this was a time when many of the conventional restraints of social life should give way to an expression of a deeper sense of brotherhood and solidarity. Dickens preached that at Christmas men should forget self and think of others, especially the poor and the unfortunate. All should participate in the great festival of brotherhood. This was the message of Dickens in his *Sketches by Boz*,

Pickwick Papers and, above all, in *A Christmas Carol*, published in 1843. The reception and continued popularity of this tale not only is a tribute to his literary skill but also suggests that its theme has an enduring appeal.

A Christmas Carol is a literary sermon against selfishness and a panegyric on brotherhood and benevolence, particularly at Christmas. It asserts that kindness and charity should be expressed at this time by all, but especially by those who have ignored or neglected these sentiments during the rest of the year. Scenes from *A Christmas Carol* are annually revived in numerous pageants throughout this country, and on nation-wide radio and television programs, and the book still has a sizable Christmas sale. Some of the characters of the story, such as Scrooge, Tiny Tim, and Bob Cratchit, have become literary stereotypes. Though the narrative involves an occasional religious reference, it is essentially secular.

The plot of *A Christmas Carol* concerns Scrooge, a merchant and financier who has hardened his heart against his fellow men, neglected his family, squeezed the poor, sacrificed his fiancée to avarice, and refused to acknowledge Christmas as a unique celebration. He is pursued in his dreams by the Spirits of Christmas Past, Present, and Future. These cause him to relive his youth and his early Christmas experiences, then to witness a Christmas celebration by his employee, Bob Cratchit and family, and that of some close relatives. Invisible, he watches the domestic celebrations of the two families and learns of his own social isolation at a time when all others are reaffirming the bonds of fellowship. Finally, the Spirit of Christmas Future forces him to witness, by prevision, his imminent death, unwept and unsung. He awakens to find that he has dreamed the story, is converted by the experience, and declares, "I will honour Christmas in my heart and try to keep it all the year."

The tale gained quick popularity in the United States and has become an important and apparently enduring part of the American Christmas. Dickens's interest in the festival continued, and in 1851 he wrote "What Christmas Is As We Grow Older," a sentimental elaboration of his earlier views. He also produced other stories for publication at Christmas, even though few of these contained any direct reference to the occasion. No other prominent writer of his century was so moved by Christmas as Dickens.

In 1868 he gave a number of public readings of *A Christmas Carol* in the United States. Of one experience he wrote:

They took it so tremendously last night that I was stopped every five minutes. One poor young girl burst into a passion of grief about Tiny Tim and had to be taken out.[33]

Popularity of the tale was so great that some people believed Dickens had invented Christmas. André Maurois has mentioned an English boy who, when told of Dickens's death, asked: "Is Mr. Dickens dead? And will Father Christmas die too?"[34]

Dickens's obsession with Christmas themes has attracted the attention of literary historians and critics. Their explanations of his personal involvement in the holiday have ranged from psychiatric analysis of his character to Marxist interpretations of his position in the "class struggles" of nineteenth century England.[35] Though these efforts are interesting, the more important question for present purposes is: Why did *A Christmas Carol* become and remain a popular part of our Christmas literature?

One answer is that nineteenth century United States was plagued by adverse social and economic conditions which could, in some instances, be grasped and dramatized through literary treatments. Poverty, slums, high death rates, and crime reflected the uneven growth of an expanding society in which industrialism and urbanism were increasing rapidly.[36] These forces concentrated population in cities which lacked adequate provision for shelter, and immigration brought a continual flow of the economically underprivileged to this country. Many of the immigrants were poorly equipped to fend for themselves. The war of 1861–1865 dislocated the national economy in important respects and placed tremendous burdens on a system still in its infancy. These conditions highlighted the disparity between the promise of our way of life and its numerous shortcomings in point of fact. Under these circumstances an increasingly humanitarian public sought remedies for social ills and welcomed the hope and warmth of Dickens's tale.

A Christmas Carol located the causes of social misery in the persistence of human greed which blinded men to their charitable duties toward others. It suggested a solution by demanding that the Scrooges of the world be convinced that the social ideals of family life, brotherhood, and benevolence transcend wealth and power. Dickens pointed the way by converting Ebenezer Scrooge under duress from a "man of business" to one "who honored Christmas in his heart" and, therefore, loved his fellow man. The enduring appeal of the story owes much to its dramatic treatment of this persistent conflict of values. At the same time it offers assurance of ultimate victory by man's "higher" nature. The conflict is couched in terms of Scrooge's spiritual struggle, but its implications extend beyond him to society. *A Christmas Carol* has become a fixture in the American festival, and is likely to persist because it deals dramatically and hopefully with this recurring human dilemma.

Some believe that Christmas was dying out about the time Dickens wrote *A Christmas Carol* and that his story revived it. Others have complained that the carol philosophy of Christmas has made people self-conscious of the occasion because they are afraid of being called "Scrooges." In any event:

Dickens certainly gave new life to the secular celebration of Christmas and did it without desecrating the religious festival.

He certainly helped enormously to universalize and democratize the Christmas celebration.[37]

By about 1870 the carol philosophy had become a basic feature of the festival. Since that time both the spirit and characters of Dickens's tale persist in the American celebration.[38] Thus the nineteenth century contributed the Dickens influence to the national celebration in addition to bringing about general ecclesiastical observance of Christmas.

The Christmas Card

During the last century the Christmas card was introduced into the United States and has become a fixture in the celebration. It had been known in England for perhaps ten or fifteen years before Louis Prang of Boston placed this type of card on the American market in 1875. He was well known as a lithographer, and produced cards of excellent quality and design, which were considered superior on both sides of the Atlantic. Prang's Christmas cards became popular immediately, and dominated the market until 1890.[39]

Designs on Prang cards included the Nativity, the visit of Santa Claus, children, young women, flowers, birds, and butterflies. Short verses, appropriate to the design, appeared on the cards.[40] Collectors of Christmas cards maintain the Prang's were superior to all others produced during the period 1875–1890. However, their superior craftsmanship and design demanded a higher price than many were willing or able to pay. About 1890, inexpensive cards began to be imported from Germany. This threatened Prang's business, since he could not meet the competition without sacrificing his standards of artistic and technical excellence, and he withdrew from the Christmas-card business about that time.

The beauty of Prang's products probably promoted the custom among the educated classes of the United States of sending greeting cards at Christmas. Once accepted, it spread rapidly among other groups when less expensive ones were available. It has become an important item in the modern celebration, and the Christmas-card list marks the initial stage of the festival.

Legal Recognition of Christmas Day

The nineteenth century increase in popularity of Christmas was demonstrated by the legal establishment of December 25th as a holiday in all states and territories between 1836 and 1890. Most states recognized several of the more popular national occasions at one time. Thus, Christmas Day, New Year's Day, Fourth of July, and Thanksgiving Day received legal recognition at the same time in many states. Alabama was the first state to acknowledge formally, in 1836, the special character of Christmas Day.

It is significant that initial legal recognition of December 25th originated in relation to economic and commercial interests. Thus, Christmas Day was first recognized as an occasion when promissory notes could not be collected. Provision was made that these must be collected on the day immediately preceding or following the holiday. In some instances judicial activities on Christmas Day were forbidden by law. Provisions for school holidays, closing of banks and offices of state governments were enacted later in the century. The table below indicates the years in which legislatures recognized December 25th. It is reasonable to assume that Christmas Day was observed as a folk and religious occasion prior to its legislative recognition.

TABLE I. DATES OF FIRST LEGAL RECOGNITION OF CHRISTMAS DAY BY
STATES AND TERRITORIES (1836-1890)

1836	Alabama	1863	Idaho
1838	Louisiana		North Dakota
	Arkansas	1864	Kentucky
1845	Connecticut	1865	Michigan
1848	Pennsylvania		Montana
1849	New York	1868	Kansas
	Virginia	1870	West Virginia
1850	Vermont		District of Columbia
	Georgia	1873	Nebraska
1851	California	1875	South Carolina
1852	Rhode Island		Indiana
1854	New Jersey	1876	New Mexico
1855	Delaware	1877	South Dakota
	Massachusetts		Missouri
1856	Minnesota	1879	Texas
1857	Ohio	1880	Mississippi
	Tennessee	1881	North Carolina
1858	Maine		Florida
1861	New Hampshire		Arizona
	Illinois	1882	Utah
	Nevada	1886	Wyoming
	Wisconsin	1888	Washington
	Colorado	1890	Oklahoma
1862	Oregon		
	Maryland		
	Iowa		

This table indicates that, in general, the older states recognized December 25th legally before those settled at a later date. However, the very first ones—Alabama, Arkansas, and Louisiana—were notable exceptions. Twenty-eight jurisdictions accorded legal recognition to Christmas Day between the years 1845 and 1865. After this period the remaining states and territories took similar action at the rate of one every year or so until 1890. Thirteen states took official action on the holiday during the Civil War years, 1861–1865.

The historical implications of these dates are not conclusive, but indicate that the middle decades of the nineteenth century saw the formal recognition of Christmas Day as a national holiday. This suggests the disappearance of Puritan opposition to the celebration and its acceptance as a folk festival. It was becoming the most popular of our national holidays, and manifested specifically American qualities in its folk aspect. One suspects that the legal recognition accorded December 25th was a sign of an emerging national self-consciousness which found symbolic expression in the Christmas festival. This idea receives slight confirmation from the fact that a large number of states recognized this day during the Civil War years when the sense of national identity attained a new intensity. Furthermore, the fact that in 1870 Congress established December 25th as a special day for the District of Columbia indicates that the celebration had attained considerable national popularity by that time.

The National Festival

By the latter part of the nineteenth century the various elements of Christmas had coalesced into a festival of great popularity and of considerable social significance. It not only embodied the import of the Nativity but also affirmed a secular faith in the durability of family ties and the importance of human brotherhood. In addition, Christmas folk imagery had become linked to patriotism. This was apparent in Thomas Nast's Civil War drawings which portrayed Santa Claus distributing presents in army camps and soldiers returning home on furloughs at Christmas.[41] Nast's pictures probably both reflected and stimulated popular identification of Christmas with American life. In addition, the nineteenth century celebration foreshadowed the commercial exploitation of the contemporary Christmas.

So far as denominational observance of the Nativity was concerned, the end of the nineteenth century found those churches which had traditionally marked the occasion continuing to hold morning services on Christmas Day. This group included the Episcopalian, Lutheran, Dutch, and German Reformed churches. In addition, Roman Catholic churches frequently observed the occasion with a midnight mass on December 24th and several masses on Christmas morning. On the other hand, the denominations once hostile to celebrating the feast began to hold services on the Sunday nearest December 25th. These included a Christmas sermon, seasonal decorations, special music, and programs in the church schools. The Presbyterians, Baptists, Methodists, and Congregationalists made up this group. Richards nicely summarizes this shift in denominational sentiment toward Christmas observance by saying, "Within the Protestant churches Christmas had emerged from its Roman Catholic associations and had been recognized as a part of the general inheritance of Christendom." [42]

Termination of the long-standing quarrel over Christmas was symptomatic of a general decline of hostility between militant Protestant and Roman Catholic groups in nineteenth century United States. One suspects that general observance of Christmas by different churches had a unifying social effect on their members, in spite of diverse ceremonies. In addition, participation in common folk aspects of the celebration probably promoted tolerance of its denominational differences. However, in the next century a new problem developed in connection with the religious character of the occasion. This concerned preservation of its spiritual significance against the encroachment of secular holiday influences. Later chapters will treat some aspects of this issue.

By the late 1800's Christmas Day had received formal legal recognition throughout the United States. In addition, school vacations were common on this occasion and many, though not all, parts of the country took a holiday from work on Christmas Day. The folk celebration included the following: limited pre-Christmas shopping, decorations in the stores, the Christmas-card custom, erection of trees in homes, use of holly, ivy, and mistletoe both in public and in private places, family reunions, the gift-bringing visit of Santa Claus, caroling, festive foods and drinks, plays, some gift exchanging by adults, and a background, real or imaginary, of winter.

The nineteenth century pattern of beliefs, customs, and values indicated trends in Christmas observance that would become dominant in the twentieth century. Thus by the latter part of the last century, the folk-secular aspects of Christmas were taking precedence over its religious ones. This was apparent in the increasing importance of the figure of Santa Claus and in greater emphasis on gifts and holiday feasting. It was evident also in the centering of the celebration, insensibly, about the home, family, and children. Even the granting of legal recognition to December 25th emphasized the importance of secular power in the festival.

The *Christmas Carol* humanitarianism of the nineteenth century preserved some of the spiritual implications of the Nativity without rejecting folk customs and festivities. It was thus congruent with both major aspects of the celebration. In addition, it expressed belief in the importance of brotherhood in spite of the American emphasis on individual achievement. Even today the Christmas theme of charity and generosity aids in preserving an important balance between fraternal and self-centered emphases in the national culture.

Thus the nineteenth century saw the crystallization of an American Christmas festival which manifested traditional elements yet reflected the contemporary social and cultural scene. Correspondingly, though the celebration has retained a measure of autonomy, its customs and beliefs have been powerfully affected by changes in American society.

CHAPTER II.

The Social Role of Santa Claus

The increasing popularity of the folk Christmas in the nineteenth century was manifested in the appearance and formalization of Santa Claus as its dominant symbol. In fact, both his historical origins and the more recent alterations in his appearance and significance reflect in interesting ways the persisting struggle between religious and secular forces for dominance in the festival. For the time being, this conflict seems to have been resolved in favor of the non-religious influences.

In his earliest American appearance Santa Claus was regarded as the patron of children and their special gift bringer. In his different national incarnations he came on December 5th, 24th, or even on the 31st. So far as the United States was concerned, by 1860 his visit was assumed to occur on the Eve of the Nativity. Indirectly, he has affected religious as well as folk aspects of the national festival.

Though Santa Claus is a creation of the literary and folk imagination, his progenitor, St. Nicholas, was an authentic historical figure who served as Bishop of Myra in the Eastern Church during the fourth century. He became very popular and was canonized in the ninth century. Careful scholarship has traced the diffusion of his cult throughout Europe.[1] However, the St. Nicholas figure from which Santa Claus developed was brought to the American colonies as a mixed religious-folk figure. He had long been popular in several European countries.

The Dutch who settled New York during the seventeenth century brought the folk cult of St. Nicholas. He remained the dominant figure of their midwinter celebration until the close of the next century.[2] In Holland, San Nicholaas was expected on the evening of December 5th, when children placed their wooden shoes by the fireplace and left hay for his horse. Wall has provided a popular account of his visit:

After nightfall, dressed in his red bishop's robes, he would appear in the sky on a beautiful white horse and, followed by his black servant, would alight on the roof tops, descend the chimneys, and fill the shoes of deserving children with sweetmeats and cookies. For children who had misbehaved, he would leave a birch rod as a sign of his displeasure.[3]

Though St. Nicholas was loved by children as their magical gift bringer, his day was also celebrated by adults in a festive spirit. It was marked by eating, drinking, merriment, and domestic good cheer. Johnston has suggested that this aspect of his festival may have roots in Roman civilization:

It is therefore by no means impossible that St. Nicholas had absorbed some characteristics of a happy, festive sort from the ancient Roman Saturnus and I am inclined to think that our modern St. Nick, Kris Kringle or Santa Claus, goes back to that ancient figure for this particular side of his character.[4]

Another attribute of St. Nicholas also suggests cultural borrowing: a diminutive term for St. Nicholas in Norway was *Nisse*, and this name also designated a small imp.[5] This may have been the basis for Clement Clarke Moore's description of St. Nicholas as a "right jolly old elf."

Tales of the coming of St. Nicholas either on December
5th or 24th prescribe different means of transportation. In
some legends he rode a white horse, while in others he came
in a small wagon.[6] Washington Irving, in his *Knickerbocker's
History of New York* (1809), also described St. Nicholas as
traveling through the skies in a wagon. Spencer has suggested that the magical travels of the good saint resemble
those of the Teutonic deity Thor. This figure reputedly rode
through the firmament in a chariot drawn by two white
goats.[7] There is no scholarly authority for the idea that he
came in a reindeer-drawn sleigh. Clement Clarke Moore employed this notion in his famous poem "A Visit from St.
Nicholas," but this appears to be an instance of literary invention and is not supported by folklore research.

In Anderson's 1810 woodcut, St. Nicholas is depicted as a
bishop.[8] He is tall, stately, dressed in a bishop's robes, holds a
purse in one hand and a birch rod in the other. Beside the
bishop stand two children; one, the Good Child, is happy
with presents, while the Bad Child has a rueful countenance
and wears a switch in his buttonhole. This is a sign of St.
Nicholas's disfavor. Words of an old Dutch verse accompany
the picture, describing him as a gift bringer:

> Saint Nicholas, my dear good friend
> To serve you ever was my end.
> If you will, now, me something give,
> I'll serve you ever while I live.

The drawing does not include the black servant who accompanied St. Nicholas on his annual visit in Holland. This figure did not appear in the American version of his visit.

By 1820 the United States possessed this tale of a popular
"saint" who visited children on December 5th, 24th, or 31st,
as a magical gift bringer. He traveled on horseback, in a
wagon, or even walked. In some accounts he came down the

chimney and placed presents in the shoes or stockings of good children and switches in those of the bad.

Transition

As the Nativity account provided the religious background for celebrating Christmas, Moore's poem "A Visit from St. Nicholas" (1822) embodied its folk character and crystallized popular notions of the visit of the gift bringer early in the nineteenth century, and its imagery has persisted to the present. It blended the traditional St. Nicholas with folk figures such as brownies and elves and provided the first step in the transition from St. Nicholas to the contemporary Santa Claus.

Moore used the names St. Nicholas and Santa Claus interchangeably, and employed the familiar "St. Nick" as well as the more formal name. His St. Nicholas was small, elfish, and dressed in fur, not in the robes of the Bishop of Myra. None of the legendary European figures such as Pelze-Nicol or Hans Trapp accompanied him. His sleigh and reindeer were small and moved through the sky magically, arriving on the eve of December 24th, not December 5th, the eve of St. Nicholas's day.

Recent research by Jones indicates that Washington Irving's *Knickerbocker's History* (1809) provided much of the lore of Santa Claus's visit which was to become current in the next decade and which was probably known to Moore by 1822.[9] Jones also points out that an 1821 issue of *The Children's Friend*, published in New York City, contained colored engravings of "Santeclaus" and verse which refers to his reindeer and sleigh. These may have been the sources of some of the fancies which Moore employed in his now famous poem.

Moore's failure to mention the Nativity in his poem is interesting because he was an ordained minister and the author

of several theological works. However, none of his other
writings bears any resemblance to this well known poem. His
authorship of this work has been questioned, but there is no
doubt about its influence on the imagery of the folk Christmas.[10]

Not long after the publication of Moore's "A Visit from
St. Nicholas," a number of American artists began to portray
the emerging figure of Santa Claus. These pictures varied
greatly until the time of Thomas Nast. An early portrayal of
Santa Claus by Sherman and Smith appeared in a New York
City magazine in 1843.[11] This engraving depicted him sitting
by a fireplace putting toys in children's stockings. He was
small, dressed in a fur coat and wore a close-fitting cap on
which a bishop's cross appeared. He also smoked a small
Dutch pipe and had a pleasant but not a jovial expression.
The caption under the picture, "Santa Claus the Night Before
New Year," indicates that gift bringing on days other than
December 24th and 25th persisted in New York City at
least until 1843.

Some doubt is entertained by specialists that the Sherman
and Smith drawing prefigures the American Santa Claus.
Weitenkampf believes that a drawing by J. G. Chapman in
1847 provided the first embodiment of the modern Santa
Claus.[12] This Santa Claus was large, wore fur-trimmed clothes,
high boots, and a feather in his cap. Weitenkampf also points
out that the various Santa Claus illustrators of the nineteenth
century failed to agree on his attributes. For instance, a
drawing by Fredericks in 1870 depicted him as resembling a
Druid priest who wore white, flowing robes, a wreath of
holly, was stern-looking, and held a glass of wine in his hand.[13]

Thomas Nast and Santa Claus

The work of Thomas Nast, the nineteenth century cartoonist, was paramount in influencing the development of the

modern conception of Santa Claus. Nast began a series of Christmas drawings for *Harper's Weekly* in 1863 which appeared almost every year until 1886. Paine traces Nast's conception of Santa Claus to Pelze-Nicol, a legendary companion of St. Nicholas. However, in Nast's early drawings Santa Claus more nearly resembles the "jolly old elf" of "A Visit from St. Nicholas."

In the picture "Santa Claus His Works" Nast formalized this figure by portraying his yearly round of activities.[14] One scene found him filling stockings with toys while, in another, he used a spyglass to discover children who should be rewarded or punished at Christmas. In still other drawings he made toys and dolls, decorated a Christmas tree, and drove his magic sleigh through the sky. He personified the children's gift bringer and resembled the "little people" of folklore.

Nast was the first American cartoonist to relate Christmas to patriotism. Some of his Christmas drawings were concerned with the Civil War. An early one showed Santa Claus distributing gifts to Union soldiers at Christmas. In another he portrayed a Northern soldier arriving home for an unexpected Christmas furlough while, in the background, Santa Claus deposited toys for the children.[15]

It is a tribute to Nast's pictures that his conception of Santa Claus became widely accepted in this country. He finally portrayed him as a large, jolly, white-bearded figure dressed in fur. By the latter part of the nineteenth century, this was the accepted stereotype of the gift bringer.

Parents of each generation confirmed the existence of this Santa Claus for their offspring. Some children doubted. Out of this doubting came one of the important episodes of Santa Claus history. In December, 1897, Francis Church, an editorial writer for the *New York Sun*, received a letter from an eight-year-old girl, named Virginia O'Hanlon, asking if there *really* was a Santa Claus. Church's reply became famous and was reprinted annually by his paper for over fifty years. He replied, in essence, that Santa Claus existed as an idea, even though he might never be seen. Church developed his thesis skillfully, suggesting that Santa Claus existed in part because people *must* believe in some such figure. He likened Santa Claus to the fairies who were never seen but whose acts proved their existence. Virginia was assured that Santa Claus would endure a thousand years "to make glad the heart of childhood." Church couched his interpretation in ornate, didactic phrases. This befitted an editor intent on preserving a child's fancy yet also obligated to the claims of reason. His editorial was a landmark in the crystallization of Christmas sentiments in this country, for it affirmed a belief dear to children and assented to by adults.

Ednah Proctor Clarke's poem "The Revolt of Santa Claus" reflected the appearance of a new element in the stereotype of the folk "saint." [16] This poem told of his decision not to make his annual visit on Christmas Eve. He felt that the emphasis on facts had become so great and imagination so weak that his visit had become meaningless. One by one, children of several nations assured him of their love and predicted universal disappointment if he failed to make the trip. He was moved by the children's pleas and decided to visit mankind again.

The fact that he was disenchanted about his annual trip gave Santa Claus a human quality previously lacking. Early in the century he belonged to the strange world of elves and fairies, but by 1900 he had changed into a gift bringer for children and was human in many respects.

By the turn of the present century, Santa Claus personified the popular spirit of Christmas which emphasized gifts, joy, and merriment. Children viewed him as their magical gift bringer and special friend. Both in music and in story, his figure was amplified and enriched so that a folk cult grew up about his annual visit. Song books of 1890, 1899, 1908, and 1916 carried such titles as: "Santa Claus Is Come to Town," "Santa Claus Last Christmas Eve," and "Old Santa Claus Sat

All Alone." [17] Short stories by Bret Harte, James Lane Allen, John Macy, Roark Bradford, and others popularized and humanized this burgeoning symbol.[18] Under such circumstances one might expect that this popular figure would be related to other aspects of American life and culture.

Santa Claus as Symbol

During the past fifty years Santa Claus has become a symbol of charity and generosity. This is evident in contemporary news accounts about him. One announced that "Santa Claus Spends Day in Chicago Loop District," and told of the adventures of a cab driver who dressed as Santa Claus and gave people free rides in his cab on Christmas Eve day. He reported that he "never had a happier Christmas." The meter of his cab carried the sign "Donations for Disabled Vets at Hines Hospital Accepted." [19] Another account described General Doolittle, a three-star army general, playing the role of Santa Claus at the Walter Reed Hospital on Christmas Day in 1947.[20] During World War II, Red Cross activities in distributing gifts at Christmas were described as follows: "Red Cross Santa Ready Over World."

In 1950 Santa Claus was appealed to in a letter published in a Boston, Massachusetts, paper. It described the plight of a family which had lost its home and possessions through fire. The headline of the story read: "Santa Told About Family Made Homeless by Fire." [21] Similar examples can be observed in urban newspapers nearly every Christmas. The symbol of Santa Claus is employed regularly to express charity, generosity, and benevolence.

To an even greater degree, the Santa Claus figure expresses affection and devotion to children. Powerful emotions center about the belief that children *ought* to have a happy Christmas. This means that they should receive gifts from

Santa Claus and have a Christmas tree, accompanied by excitement and the affection of adults. The importance of Santa Claus is evident in Christmas headlines: "G.I.'s to Play Santa to German Children"; "Santa at Hospital Party"; "Santa Claus Calls on Boys and Girls at Temporary Home." This is repeated year after year.

The importance of Santa Claus as the gift bringer is so great that many adults believe children have a "right" to expect him and to "have a happy Christmas." This holds true even if the celebration is not held on December 25th. A story which appeared in September, 1947, illustrates this. The headline read, "Child [name omitted] Dies Awaiting Santa Claus."

With death so near, her parents decided to give her a final Christmas party. They set up a gaily decorated tree by her bed and told her Santa Claus would arrive next Saturday [September 25th] but the child died in her sleep this morning.[22]

In the same year another afflicted child "greeted" Santa Claus in October because medical authorities had advised his parents that he would not live until Christmas.[23] The concern that ill children should "have their Christmas" and "get presents from Santa Claus" suggests that this experience is considered a "natural right" of children. The appeal of Santa Claus was revealed in another manner in 1945. A war orphan living in an institution wrote to him asking for a *real* home. The letter was publicized, and over a hundred families indicated willingness to offer a home to the child. Orphanage authorities couched their appeal for help in these terms: "We've just got to find homes or *deny the Santa Claus legend.*" [24]

An elaborate effort to preserve faith in the cherished folk tale took form in the Santa Claus Association, organized in 1914 by John D. Gluck in New York City. Its declared purpose was "to preserve children's faith in Santa Claus." [25] This agency planned to obtain letters addressed to Santa Claus from the postal authorities and to investigate them. If need appeared, individual donors of the association would provide toys and presents for the writers. Sometimes the association paid rent for destitute families, but it maintained that its chief objective was to preserve children's faith in Santa Claus. The association operated in New York City from 1914 to 1928.

Similar organizations developed in several other large American cities. In 1928 the Federal postal authorities refused to permit letters addressed to Santa Claus to be turned over to the Santa Claus Association. The organization was investigated and criticized. In defense of his policies Mr. Gluck said, "All I ask is that these people don't sock it to us at this time of the year and spoil the faith of little children." [26]

Commercial Uses of Santa Claus

Modern advertising and merchandising have used Santa Claus for financial gain. Many persons believe that commercial use of this figure and the emphasis on gift exchanging have "spoiled" or "ruined" Christmas. Though this may be true for some individuals, business exploitation of Christmas has actually increased interest in the folk celebration. Pre-Christmas advertisements make frequent reference to Santa Claus to attract the attention of buyers. A department store asserted in a half-page advertisement, "This year's Santa is shopping at ———," while another firm of national reputation insisted that "of course ——— has the real Santa Claus." The Western Union Telegraph Company placed a messenger's cap on Santa Claus in a December, 1950, advertisement.[27] He was shown pointing to special Western Union Christmas messages with manifest approval. Department stores in large cities have installed special telephone lines so that children can talk to Santa. Chambers of Commerce usually include him in their municipal Christmas decorations.

A wide variety of commercial agencies—department stores, banks, investment firms, and so on—employ the symbol of Santa Claus to promote business activity. The continued use of this figure, year after year, demonstrates its commercial value and has resulted in an ever wider knowledge of the gift bringer. Santa Claus is certainly more popular with contemporary children than he was in 1900.

The use of "real" Santas by many retail stores has done much to stereotype the figure. The *New York Times* commented in 1927:

A standardized Santa Claus appears to New York children. Height, weight, stature are almost exactly standardized, as are the red garments, the hood and the white whiskers. The pack full of toys, ruddy cheeks and nose, bushy eyebrows and a jolly, paunchy effect are also inevitable parts of the requisite make-up.[28]

In general, this description characterizes the contemporary Santa Claus.

Standardization of the figure and the increasing commercial demand for Santa Clauses has undoubtedly led to the development of several "schools" for training Santas. One of these was established by Charles W. Howard of Albion, New York. His course of instruction is designed for those aspiring to play the role of Santa Claus in department stores or to appear at hospital parties, benefits, and other public occasions. The training program includes indoctrination in the history of the Santa Claus legend, dressing for the role, wearing beards, dealing with children, and acquiring a general familiarity with the role of the professional Santa Claus.

A new type of Christmas organization came into existence in 1943 named "Santa's Helpers." [29] This firm provided visits by Santa Claus to individual children, to children's parties, schools, clubs, and so on. Those who purchase its services must supply advance information on the family or group to be visited, thus enabling the professional Santa Claus to play his role with some degree of familiarity with both people and surroundings.

About 1947 a toy factory was opened at Upper Jay, New York, which bore the name "North Pole—Home of Santa's Workshop." Later this establishment was expanded to include a toyland with such attractions as reindeer, a professional Santa Claus, sheep, a toy train, and numerous items to appeal to the young. It is one of the more elaborate examples of the commercial exploitation of Santa Claus folklore.

Frequent use of the professional Santa Claus sometimes confuses children who encounter several different ones in a single day. The City Council of Boston asked the Mayor in 1948 to "permit only one Santa in the city in 1949 and to station him on the historic Boston Common." [30] One council member asserted that "there is a Santa on every corner and children are beginning to wonder." Use of the figure of Santa Claus by commercial artists was attacked in a bill introduced in the California Senate in 1939. Senator Westover declared:

Santa Claus primarily belongs to the children, but commercial artists have used his figure to such an extent that he is depicted selling everything from bottled beer to automobiles.[31]

The clash of folk beliefs and economic philosophies is amusingly illustrated by an episode which occurred in Muskegon, Michigan, in 1949. A local savings bank decided to advertise the virtues of thrift on billboards. It erected one during the Christmas season which carried the message: THERE IS NO SANTA CLAUS—WORK—EARN—SAVE. This denial of the existence of Santa Claus aroused so much protest from parents that the bank was forced to alter its advertisement.

The president of the bank declared: "The myth of Santa Claus is far-reaching and implies a nation of people who seem to accept a Santa Claus with headquarters at Washington."[32]

A town in Indiana which acquired the name "Santa Claus" in the 1890's has recently turned it to profitable use by erecting a forty-foot municipal statue of him. Thousands of children visit the town annually to see the statue, and a large volume of mail is sent to the local post office each year for remailing in order to obtain the local cancellation. Rival business interests have engaged in quarrels and litigation over sites and trade names in the city of Santa Claus. A new extreme in the commercialization of Christmas symbols was attempted by a firm which sought incorporation under the laws of Indiana as "Christmas With Santa Claus, Santa Claus, Indiana." State officials refused, declaring:

Santa Claus is either a geographical name, a post office address in this state, or it is the name of a mythical being. It is such a name in strict justice and law that it cannot be the subject of an exclusive proprietorship.[33]

For and Against Santa Claus

There is abundant evidence that Santa Claus is enormously important to the American Christmas and has become the central figure of the folk celebration, comparable in importance to the Christ Child in the Nativity. He appears each year in music, literature, and pictures throughout the entire country. In addition, his cult has spread to other parts of the world with remarkable rapidity. Children regard him with a mixture of admiration and awe, even though some of the young shrink from a physical confrontation of a professional Santa Claus.[34] Adults appear determined to preserve the "faith" of young children in the gift bringer and to attack critics of the secular "saint."

Periodically, well known public figures express their views on the Santa Claus myth. In 1923 *Collier's Weekly* asked eighteen well known writers for their opinions of him. The group included Joseph Conrad, H. G. Wells, James Branch Cabell, and H. L. Mencken. Eight asserted a fervid belief in the desirability of the myth, five were neutral, and five opposed it.[35] Statements varied from G. B. Shaw's "Santa Claus be blowed" to Booth Tarkington's moderate "I think that children should be permitted to preserve their happy illusions as long as possible."

Some years later a group of American women artists were interviewed concerning their belief in the existence of Santa Claus. Their reactions were strongly in the affirmative. An article summarizing their views was headed "You Can't Tell Some People There Is No Santa Claus." One of the group said: "I never stopped believing." [36]

Other champions of Santa Claus have asserted faith in "his" existence and have defended the conspiracy of adults to preserve belief in him on grounds of possible benefits to children. Judge John H. Hatcher of the West Virginia Supreme Court was one of these. In 1927 he issued an opinion entitled *"Ex parte Santa Claus"* from his court.[37] Judge Hatcher attacked both those who sought to alter the popular conception of the person and visit of Santa Claus and those who wanted to abandon the tale. In concluding his defense of the gift bringer, the judge asserted:

Let legislation outlaw the law of evolution, if they must; let the Constitution be amended till it looks like a patchwork quilt; but rob not childhood of its most intriguing mystery—Santa Claus. Let him be to succeeding generations as he has been to us—a joyous faith of childhood, a pleasant indulgence of parenthood and a happy memory of old age.[38]

Judge Hatcher's defense of Santa Claus resembles that of Francis Church's editorial. He insisted that children want and need the Santa Claus symbol, asserted the value of imaginary figures, and derided those who demand proof of his existence. In opposing changes in the traditional Santa Claus, Judge Hatcher resembled most parents, who want to transmit their childhood memories of Santa Claus unchanged to their children. Parents probably seek to link their children to themselves through meaningful folklore symbols which may bind generations in spite of different occupations and social philosophies.

On December 23, 1936, Judge M. A. Musmanno of the Allegheny County Criminal Court of Pennsylvania ruled doubters of Santa Claus in contempt of court. Judge Musmanno issued the following statement to support belief in the existence of Santa Claus:

. . . Santa Claus is not a figment of the imagination. He is actuality. Santa Claus is the symbol of kindness; he is the token of smiling charity; he is the badge of all that is cheerfully benevolent in the make up of man.[39]

This public official also asserted that the existence of the "idea" of Santa Claus was evidence of his "actual" existence. This effort to perpetuate beliefs in mythical beings in a society which prides itself on being "hardheaded" and "practical" is significant. It suggests a deep need for occasional excursions into the worlds of fantasy and make-believe. Both jurists employed deadpan humor in their attempts to reconcile reality with the claims of fantasy. Perhaps they shared the feelings of Gamaliel Bradford, who wrote:

The fairies are gone. . . . The witches are gone . . . the ghosts are gone. Santa Claus alone still lingers with us. For Heaven's sake let us keep him as long as we can.[40]

Even though the figure of Santa Claus has become very popular, he has been attacked a number of times. As early as 1903 the Santa Claus myth was criticized in an editorial in the *New York Daily Tribune*.[41] In addition, occasional hostility toward the gift bringer was expressed from time to time in the pulpit and the press. In recent years public objections to Santa Claus have been made by religious leaders and occasionally by psychiatrists.

Wilbur Glenn Voliva, head of the Catholic Apostolic Church of Zion City, Illinois, barred Santa Claus from that city in 1921.[42] He instructed his followers to tell their children that gifts came from above. The Reverend C. E. Wagner warned his congregration in a sermon delivered in December of 1927 that "Santa Claus will crowd out Christ."[43] The Reverend Del A. Fehsenfeld, pastor of the Argentine Baptist Church in Kansas City, Kansas, denounced Santa Claus from the pulpit as "a dirty lie." When Pastor Fehsenfeld defended his actions in a court hearing in 1950, he remarked:

Some people are more interested in teaching their children there is a Santa Claus and an Easter Bunny than in teaching about the Virgin Birth and the Resurrection. To teach your children it is a fact that there is a Santa Claus is to lie.[44]

Another minister, the Reverend Martin F. Clough, denounced the teaching of a belief in the existence of Santa Claus in these words:

Santa is the most popular hoax of the age. Around the globe so-called Christian parents are deceiving the children about Santa Claus. Santa Claus is a modern representative of the heathen god Nimrod who is a defiant hater of God and Satan's earliest effort to produce Anti-Christ.[45]

In 1949, the Reverend John Sinnott Martin, a Catholic editor, asserted that "Santa the Saint" had become "Santa the Sugar Daddy."

Many children are so steeped in the commercialized version of Christmas that the ox and the ass, the true symbols of the Nativity, have been crowded from their thoughts by visions of gift-bearing reindeer dancing across the roof tops.[46]

He also criticized the teaching of Santa Claus's existence on other grounds, and insisted that children's eventual disillusionment about Santa Claus would injure them emotionally, destroy family discipline and the influence of the church.

In spite of these dissenting voices, the major religious denominations appear disinclined to attack the figure of Santa Claus or to deny the story of his visit. Rather, they have emphasized the Nativity tale and the Christian character of the occasion. Churches adjust their celebrations to the competing symbols of Santa Claus and the gift-laden Christmas tree according to local conviction and custom.

Santa Claus continues to be the chief, if not the only, gift bringer in the national Christmas. In spite of the fact that gifts were reputedly brought by the Christ Child in Germany and by *le petit Jésu* in France during the nineteenth century, this legend has not achieved popularity in the United States. Perhaps this was due to the initial opposition of the Puritans and others to the religious celebration of the occasion. These groups would have found the idea of the Christ Child as a gift bringer repugnant, but were, perhaps, able to accept the secular St. Nick in the same role. Today American churches utilize the figure of Santa Claus to distribute gifts at Christmas parties held after religious services.

In all probability Santa Claus—the popular gift bringer —has protected the figure of Christ from commercial influences. He is a symbol congruent with the secular spirit of the occasion and is traditionally associated with children, gifts, and acquisitiveness. His figure can be used in advertising, store decorations, and promotional devices without affronting religious sentiments. As a result, representations of Christ seldom appear in a commercial context at Christmas. This affords a measure of protection for the ecclesiastical celebration against encroachments of secular influences and covetousness.

In 1945 a well known psychiatrist, Dr. Brock Chisholm, attacked the Santa Claus tale. He said:

Any child who believes in Santa Claus has had his ability to think permanently injured. Such a child will become the kind of man who will develop a sore back when there is a tough job to do and refuse to think realistically when war threatens.[47]

Dr. Chisholm interprets belief in Santa Claus as a flight from reality which encourages children to develop passive attitudes toward life. Consequently, they tend to assume that their wants will always be answered and that help will come from some magical source. Chisholm believes the figure of Santa Claus promotes such emotional dependence on a wide scale.

However, he does not offer clinical findings to support his interpretation, though his professional reputation warrants a respectful hearing. Other specialists have expressed dissimilar views concerning the effects of this story on the human personality.[48] The lay person is inclined to believe that the impact of the folk tale on individuals will vary enormously and will depend on the circumstances under which children become acquainted with the figure of Santa Claus. This involves such matters as the particular persons who introduce it to the child, relations with his parents, and his basic personality.

Gesell has asserted that normal children accept and use the Santa Claus story in accordance with their emotional needs and in relation to their age and mental development.[49] His view suggests that children are not passive recipients of the tale, but confront it on their own terms. There is inadequate evidence to support the causal relationship inferred by Chisholm between belief in Santa Claus and emotional dependency.

Recently Sereno has attacked Santa Claus on somewhat different psychological grounds. He believes that adults indoctrinate children with belief in Santa Claus because they experience chronic anxiety about being worthy of love and affection.[50] In the case of parents, this insecurity is masked by using the figure of Santa Claus to express love for their children through the medium of gifts. The ambiguous character of parental love appears in attempts to control children by threats of withholding presents if they misbehave. Thus, adult emotional needs are chiefly responsible for perpetuating the Santa Claus myth and customs. He goes so far as to say, "Children have little or nothing to do with the Santa Claus practice, and they are often involved in it against their will." [51]

To support this thesis, Sereno described a group of twenty children of kindergarten age who were taken to a department store to meet Santa Claus:

They approached him with patent discomfort, obviously because they saw no reason for disclosing their wishes to a stranger. . . . A few children recognized the person who was playing Santa, and though a bit relieved, they refused to be hoodwinked by his travesty. Other children were too scared to approach him, broke into tears, and were finally pushed to his stand.[52]

This account is certainly at variance with the experience of many parents and does not accord with other reports.[53] Though some children experience fright at their first physical contact with a "professional" Santa Claus, others accept it with pleasure and look forward to the event each year. If any significant proportion of the American children who annually meet Santa Claus should find the experience harrowing, the practice would shortly be discontinued. This would be done in the interests of business profits, if not of the mental health of the young. In any event, the tale has wider significance for the young than that acquired by confronting the gift bringer in the flesh.

In addition, parents and teachers have long noticed that children obtain many of their impressions of the character and meaning of Santa Claus from their playmates. They elaborate these spontaneously, without regard to adult interpretations, and invest the tale with meanings appropriate to their stage of mental and emotional development. Children do not react to the Santa Claus account as the submissive victims of unrecognized needs in adults.

Sereno's original explanation of the forces perpetuating the Santa Claus custom rests, also, on a questionable psychological assumption. Though some adults experience chronic anxiety concerning love and affection, there are no adequate grounds for characterizing an entire people and generation in this manner. His evidence on this issue is so fragmentary as to raise doubts about the interpretation. There are other explanations of the perpetuation of this folk tale which are more nearly consonant with cultural history and the character of contemporary society.

Santa Claus in American Culture

So far as historical affinities were concerned, the American Santa Claus resembled earlier European figures such as St. Nicholas and Knecht Rupprecht, who were familiar to early German and Dutch colonists. In addition, the elfish qualities of the American gift bringer may have encouraged the Irish in the United States to accept him because he was like the "little people" of their folklore. Americans of Scandinavian origins also found him not very different from folk figures of their native countries. In addition, Santa Claus was similar, in some respects, to the traditional English "Father Christmas,"

England

who personified the secular gaiety and feasting that occurred on Christmas Eve. Thus, his ready acceptance in the United States undoubtedly reflects the fact that he developed from familiar European and British antecedents. However, this fails to explain his growing importance.

There are some historical clues to alterations in the character of Santa Claus which may account for his increasingly dominant role in Christmas. The period after 1850 in particular emphasized individual success and material wealth and attached great importance to these symbols for all classes.[54] As this occurred, children began to expect more lavish gifts from Santa Claus, and he gradually became the symbol of abundant material wealth. Parents learned, often with surprise, that their childhood Christmas presents were inadequate, as judged by demands of a later generation. This disparity prevails today between the gift expectations of different generations.

America

His historical role as a gift bringer also made it comparatively easy for Santa Claus to become a national symbol of affluence and generosity. Thus a business economy, guided by the profit motive and geared to mass consumption, found Santa Claus a useful promotional tool because he personified material bounty, good will, and generosity. For this reason stores were able to use him quite effectively in promoting Christmas business.

In still other ways Santa Claus mirrored important social currents of the past century. Public concern for children resulted in the enactment of protective legislation for them and in the establishment of child welfare agencies. Parallel to these developments, Santa Claus appeared increasingly as the patron of children and assumed a place of central importance in their experience. Adults nurtured this notion by asserting that children possess a "right" to enjoy Christmas and to receive gifts from Santa Claus.

The changing significance of this figure is apparent in the

literary and pictorial treatment of his character and behavior. In most of these he is depicted as concerned chiefly with children. To them he is permissive, generous, and forgiving. Thus American children seldom doubt that they will receive presents at Christmas in spite of warnings by adults about the necessity of good behavior. Santa Claus continues his annual trips for the children's sake, and though he admonishes them about their conduct, he always does so in a gentle, loving manner.

Paradoxically, he appears androgynous in spite of his conventional masculine dress. This suggests the possibility that Santa Claus has acquired feminine and, particularly, maternal characteristics. This development in his character may be related to recent changes in American life and culture. For example, within the past century women have achieved political, economic, and social rights and privileges formerly denied them, and are generally believed to exert a preponderant influence in child rearing and family life. The disciplining of children is carried out increasingly by mothers, and the direct influence of fathers on offspring is declining, especially in the urban middle classes.[55] As the influence of women has grown greater in this country, it may have affected even the folk figure of Santa Claus by introducing feminine qualities into his character and appearance.

Though he is considered the patron of children, adults do much to maintain and transmit the tale of Santa Claus from generation to generation. As children they readily accept the belief in the gift bringer, but eventually discover its fictional character. Nevertheless, in their later roles as parents, they conspire in perpetuating it. In this respect, there is substance to Sereno's insistence that the story concerns parents chiefly, even though his explanation of this is open to question.

Children learn the Santa Claus story through parents, other adults, playmates, and by songs, stories, and pictures. It contains the figure of the gift bringer, his visit on Christmas Eve, reindeer, magical powers, and emphasizes affection for children. The significance of the tale varies with every child because it reflects the attitudes of those who familiarize him with it, as well as his personality needs. This means that though the cultural content of the story remains relatively fixed, its psychological significance varies somewhat for each child.

Sereno has referred to the story of the gift bringer as the "Santa Claus custom." This is a useful characterization because it denotes the attitudes of most parents toward the belief and defines their relation to it. Furthermore, children of the last seventy-five years have, for the most part, acquired familiarity with the person and visit of Santa Claus as a normal part of their social experience. Later, as parents, they consider it a duty to transmit the story to their children as a significant part of American childhood culture. Undoubtedly parents differ widely in their estimate of the importance of this indoctrination and as to the manner in which it should be carried out. Continued belief in Santa Claus beyond the age of eight or nine is viewed as a sign of social naïveté in a child. Adults who are consistently over-optimistic are said to "believe in Santa Claus."

One suspects that the efforts of most parents to introduce their children to the department-store Santa Claus demonstrates chiefly their desire to have their offspring acquire the standard cultural knowledge of their age group. Familiarity with Santa Claus is considered evidence that their youngster is a "normal American child." This interpretation throws some light on the conflict experienced by Jewish parents over the Santa Claus tale. They are undecided whether to encourage their children to accept Santa Claus as a communal folk figure or to view all aspects of Christmas as somehow a part of the Nativity celebration. Their problem is that rejecting the story of the gift bringer is tantamount, in some respects, to renouncing an important part of the culture of the dominant group in the United States. In this sense, acceptance of Santa Claus is an indication of assimilation, as Sereno has shrewdly pointed out.[56]

It should not be overlooked that parents may make deliberate use of the Santa Claus figure to mask their motives and behavior in Christmas giving. Some wish their children to have lavish Christmas presents, but consider too great parental generosity unwise. For them the figure of the gift bringer is a convenient one on which to project this responsibility. On the other hand, parents in reduced circumstances may find it expedient to attribute the poverty of their gifts to the inscrutable ways of Santa Claus.

Not all persons passively accept the Santa Claus story as a necessary part of childhood culture. There are parents who consider it harmful, and early disabuse their children of popular notions concerning the gift bringer. Some children accept the parental dictum that "there isn't any Santa Claus," but others find the tale too attractive to deny or abandon. Apparently their unconscious emotional needs often call for a magical helper, such as Santa Claus, and they are unable to tolerate a denial of his existence even when it proceeds from their parents. Still other children are introduced to the account in "reality" terms: they are told that it is a fictional tale about an imaginary character and that people "pretend" to believe the story. This enables the parent to acquaint the child with an important symbol without imputing a quality of real existence to it.

Many parents are uneasy when faced with the necessity of admitting to their children that Santa Claus is an unreal figure. In part this is due to their reluctance to acknowledge that they have lied. Since American cultural norms generally forbid lying, yet prescribe it under some circumstances, this confused attitude is understandable. Further, the normal parent may worry lest his child suffer keen disappointment on learning the truth about Santa Claus. If the parent suffered such unhappiness in his own childhood, this may very well intensify his sense of conflict about disillusioning his children.

Perhaps the reluctance of parents to disillusion their children about Santa Claus also affords another insight into the nature of this symbol and its role in American culture. The figure of the gift bringer has import beyond the world of children, domestic affection, charity, and business. He has also come to signify an optimistic secular faith which assumes an abundance of material goods and the continuing possibility of unexpected good fortune for all. This hopeful view of human life persists as an essential aspect of American culture and tends to be accepted even by those who have never "gotten the breaks." Since Santa Claus personifies this inner core of optimism in national life, parents are understandably reluctant to deny his existence to their children. Such an admission would symbolically deny an important article of faith in American culture. Few persons are prepared to take this step without qualms.

The conclusion seems inescapable that Santa Claus has become the key figure of the folk celebration of Christmas and is a symbol with which most Americans must come to terms at some time in their lives. In addition to his clear dominance of the secular Christmas, Santa Claus has even penetrated some phases of the religious observance. Thus, in some Christian churches, a Santa Claus figure gives presents to children after Christmas religious services are completed. This is done on church premises, though not within the church building. Perhaps this practice indicates a slight ecclesiastical concession to the popularity of the children's patron, or it may signify only a blurring of lines between the religious and folk celebrations brought about by the impact of secularization on all aspects of American culture.

CHAPTER III.

Christmas in Church, Family, and School

Evidence of the gradual drift toward the secularization of Christmas is apparent in the holiday activities of important social groups in contemporary United States. For example, though churches, families, schools, charitable agencies, and business firms celebrate the festival, invariably they do so in a manner calculated to express and preserve their special group interests. This is true, in a sense, even of the Christian churches, which consciously use the occasion to appeal both to members and to others for support and participation in their activities. Thus, considerations such as the number who attend Christmas services and the amount of money contributed by the congregation are emphasized sometimes more than the spiritual significance of the occasion.

Furthermore, it is evident that the business community exploits the occasion for gain, and other important social groups use both sacred and temporal elements of the festival to serve their special ends. This deliberate manipulation of important traditional celebrations is characteristic of secularization, and has altered Christmas in ways that may decisively affect its character. An examination of this process may well begin with the contemporary role of the Christian church in Christmas.

The Church

In contrast to the Puritan opposition to Christmas, the contemporary ecclesiastical celebration has become very prominent in Christian churches and is rivaled in importance only by Easter.[1] Each year sees a multiplicity of religious services and activities oriented to the Nativity theme. Some denominations also encourage spiritual preparation for Christmas through special services which begin with Advent and continue until Epiphany.* Both religious workers and lay persons believe that church attendance increases sharply during this season. This is particularly true on Christmas Eve and Christmas Sunday.

Most Christian denominations make elaborate preparations to observe Christmas and try to attract public attention to their services.[2] For example, newspapers often devote full pages to information about forthcoming Christmas services, pictures of the Nativity, and musical offerings during the pre-Christmas period. The addresses of churches appear in notices, and many of these even specify available transportation routes.

Protestant church schools use special lesson materials during the Christmas season, and most religious services deal with some aspect of the Nativity. The majority of Christian groups emphasize the virtue of the "giving" Christmas in contrast to the secular stress on "getting" through gift exchanging. In order to emphasize this view, Phebe A. Curtis wrote a special Christmas service entitled "White Gifts for the King," which involved the presentation by children of white-wrapped gifts at a Christmas religious service. Symbolically, these presents were birthday gifts for Jesus as well as contributions to the needy. This practice spread rapidly in Protestant circles and is

---

* Advent is the season including the four Sundays before December 25th. Epiphany is observed on January 6th.

used extensively today to assist in preserving the religious significance of the occasion.

An important consequence of the annual Nativity observance is that the services bring together those already linked by common ties of belief and sentiment. They encounter the emotional appeal of music and of liturgy, and receive social stimulation as well. Consequently Christmas services not only symbolize the religious importance of the occasion but also provide a unifying social experience for the participants. This is particularly true of families, some of which attend church as a group only at Christmas and perhaps at Easter. Participation in these collective rituals may strengthen family solidarity as well as maintain bonds between church and home.

As a matter of fact, the Christmas festival provides Christian churches an excellent opportunity for identifying religious interests and family affairs. In the entire year there is no other time when these so easily converge. This is due to the fact that the Nativity theme naturally arouses and stimulates family sentiments because it epitomizes our idealized version of parental affection and the mutual devotion of father and mother. To an unusual degree, it expresses unalloyed family feelings, with special interest centered on the Child.

In so far as the religious observance evokes sentiments which are also idealized in secular aspects of our culture, it thereby secures strength for its own rituals and tends to integrate different realms of values. For example, the humble surroundings of the manger at Bethlehem provide an atmosphere of humility and brotherhood which is also congruent with American sympathy for the poor and the oppressed. As a result, the annual display of manger scenes in thousands of churches and homes both strengthens the appeal of this tale and reinforces humanitarianism in American culture. Thus Christmas religious ritual has a powerful effect

in maintaining common values in our society. Furthermore, it
is interesting to note that the gift-bringing visit of the Wise
Men and the presence of animals in the manger scene bear
some resemblance to the later visit of Santa Claus to the children. Here, again, the Nativity imagery has influenced secular
culture.

However, Christmas religious pronouncements on brotherhood and peace high-light the frequent differences between
social ideals and actual behavior. Thus Christianity extols
human brotherhood and peace, but American society does
not consistently exemplify these values in practice. On the
contrary, the American application of the principle of
brotherhood is often restricted to the white race, and though
peace is considered desirable it is not an ultimate value in
our society. Daily life exhibits socially approved struggle, conflict, and hostility, though fraternity, kindness, and cooperation are not lacking. Actual behavior simply does not conform to these Christian ideals in very many instances.

Even though these Christian values are frequently ignored
or violated, they are not without influence on contemporary
society. They are widely diffused throughout American
culture as guides to exemplary conduct, and their inculcation
begins early in home, church, and school and is continuous.
However, these values are in conflict with others, such as
survival, success, class and racial privileges, and are often
subordinated to them. As a result, there are frequent viola-
tions of these Christian ideals which give rise to feelings of
guilt in many persons.

In these circumstances Christmas religious ceremonies offer
an opportunity to lessen this sense of failure by providing
rituals which extol the neglected goals of peace and brotherhood. The need for diminishing guilt varies among individuals
and also reflects prevailing social conditions at a particular
time. Paradoxically, the greatest emphasis on peace occurs at
Christmas religious services held during war years.[3]

Not infrequently lay groups demonstrate spontaneous interest in the religious character of the Christmas season. In Neosho, Missouri, in December, 1947, for example, a local group decided to hold morning services during the pre-Christmas period.[4] They were trying to come closer to the "spiritual meaning" of the Nativity, and planned to meet for half an hour every morning at seven-fifteen, expecting perhaps fifty to attend. Instead, their church was packed every morning with as many as 350 men attending in overalls and business suits. The attorney who initiated the venture said, "It's hard to explain, but this Christmas in Neosho has more meaning than any we can remember." Of course, this isolated instance does not demonstrate general public concern for the spiritual significance of the Nativity, but such accounts appear frequently at Christmas. They suggest that Christian tradition and imagery are fundamental to the occasion in spite of secular holiday forces.

One contemporary Christian group, Jehovah's Witnesses, opposes the celebration of Christmas, regarding it as an admixture of Christian and pagan customs.[5] They condemn Christmas gifts as contrary to the spirit of original Christianity. This group also opposes the tree and festive lights. Their objections are directed chiefly at the intrusion of pagan and commercial elements into the religious festival rather than at the celebration of the Nativity. In a like manner Mary Baker Eddy, founder of the Christian Science faith, accepted the religious celebration of Christmas but objected to the inclusion of Santa Claus in the festival.[6] Both Jehovah's Witnesses and Mrs. Eddy object to the secularization of Christmas, not to its religious observance.

In spite of the fact that Jews do not, of course, accept the Christian significance of the Nativity, the celebration of Christmas concerns them. The ubiquity of the folk Christmas and the blurred distinctions between the religious and folk aspects of the festival have embarrassed some Jewish groups

settled in predominantly gentile communities. Especially
where carol singing has been practiced in public schools at
Christmas, a difficult question faces Jewish families. Should
they participate in this gentile religious observance? One rabbi
has publicly approved the celebration of the folk—not the
religious—Christmas by Jews:

I say, then, as a rabbi, thank God for Christmas. May it, in the
spirit of its Judaeo-Christian founder bring forth in ever fuller
measure the love that is hidden in the hearts of men until, like
a flood, it prevails over the face of the earth.[7]

On the other hand, a Jew writing in the *Reconstructionist* in
1948 explained some basic points of difference between
Jewish and Christian views of Christ, and said:

I hope you will understand now why we Jews cannot believe in
Santa Claus or inhale with satisfaction the Christ-has-come atmosphere of the Christmas season.[8]

A group of Jewish war veterans in New Jersey revealed
another attitude toward Christmas by volunteering to supply
substitute workers for Christians who would otherwise be
unable to have a holiday on December 25th. No conditions
were attached to the offer, and no compensation was expected
for the work. A spokesman for the group said that the offer
was an effort "to express our gratitude for the splendid relationship that exists between the Jewish members of our community and our Christian neighbors."[9] Here the Christmas
festival offered an occasion in which a Jewish group demonstrated a sense of tolerance strong enough to promote indirect
support of a celebration it did not observe.

It is ironic that efforts to maintain community solidarity
occur at Christmas. Ideally, this occasion should banish
awareness of differences of race, color, and creed, but actually it tends to sharpen social distinctions between Chris-

tians and Jews. This is certainly an unintended consequence of observing the natal day of Jesus—a symbol of brotherhood. It demonstrates that fraternally motivated actions may be the means of perpetuating prevailing social differences instead of eliminating them.

In non-religious respects, the Jewish group has tended to conform to the accepted meaning and customs of the Christmas festival. This is exemplified by the fact that many of its members adhere to an important social value of the festival—that of generosity—indicating a latent kind of conformity to the occasion. It is also exhibited in the adoption by many Jews of the Christmas tree and the Christmas-card custom.

Religious Opposition to Secularizing Christmas

Though nearly all Christian churches now celebrate Christmas, its religious character is threatened by secular holiday influences. Commercial manipulation of the occasion is partly responsible for this condition, but other factors are also involved. The figure of Santa Claus is ubiquitous during the pre-Christmas season, and there is great stress on gift exchanging. Public interpretation of the period is chiefly in terms of merriment, joy, and even license. A clerical critic of the contemporary secular Christmas has asserted:

Christmas to the vast throngs is little more than a noisy excuse for meretricious salesmanship, for urging one and all to buy unwanted presents for their friends, to the profit of the dollar hungry. For a month before the Feast, the cry is: Buy . . . Adeste Fideles . . . Nylons for your lady . . . It Came Upon a Midnight Clear. What came, Mummy? Santa Claus, my darling.[10]

Many churches have resisted the secular appropriation of the occasion, but without marked success. A Methodist church in Indiana recently tried to circumvent the commercial note at Christmas by celebrating the Nativity during the month of July. The church was equipped with a manger, a Christmas tree was placed on the lawn, and food was served in the social rooms. There were no gifts, but collections were taken for several charities. The celebration originated with lay members of the church, and the minister declared: "It's a splendid idea because of the motive behind it . . . the spirit of Christmas is something that need not be confined to the holiday season.[11]

John J. Thomas, S.J., discovered that secular Christmas customs diminish awareness of the religious significance of the occasion. He made a study which attempted to evaluate the results of religious instruction received by preschool children in Catholic homes. The child's grasp of the meaning of Christmas was used as one index of his understanding of the teachings of his church. Thomas remarks:

The story of Christmas is one which children grasp very readily, and the ritual of the church on this feast is so elaborate that it is difficult to understand how they could forget the story, provided that the parents had made some effort to explain it. However, as one teacher remarked, "No matter how I put the question, the same answer comes back: Christmas meant only Santa Claus and gifts!" [12]

Apparently there are grounds for concern lest attractions of the folk aspect of the festival lead to neglect of its religious character.

A dramatic instance of religious resistance to the secularization of Christmas occurred in Milwaukee, Wisconsin, in 1949.

More than 200 Milwaukee merchants launched a cooperative drive sparked by the "Milwaukee Archconfraternity of Christian Mothers," a Roman Catholic group which has already plastered city busses and street cars with 1200 posters bearing its slogan: "Put Christ back into Christmas." Starting Dec. 11, some 275 taxicabs will display pictures of the Nativity. Hotel and theater marquees will carry the slogan, as will 160 billboards and daily radio and TV announcements. This campaign was backed by Lutherans, Episcopalians and by many Jews who feel that Christmas should be restored to its original religious meaning.[13]

There is no doubt that the religious character of Christmas in the United States is maintained with some difficulty and that it will continue to be threatened by secular emphases. However, it must be remembered that midwinter folk festivals are very ancient and were early approved by the Christian Church as appropriate at the Christmas season.[14] Practices of feasting, visiting, mumming, drinking, gift exchanging, and reveling were rooted in pre-Christian winter festivals such as the Roman Saturnalia and the Kalends of January. These persisted for many centuries, often with a degree of church tolerance and approval. Though these secular celebrations were later overshadowed by the Christian Nativity, especially in the Latin countries, they persisted in the Germanic countries. As the United States acquired a larger German population, toleration of the folk celebration increased.

The decline in the strictly religious significance of the occasion is but one evidence of the secularization occurring in this country during the past century. Rationality and science have diminished the hold of religion on men's minds and have made possible the acquisition of new material satisfactions. These developments have been paralleled by a decline in religious influences in American culture, even though church membership has kept pace with population growth. At the present time about 55 per cent of the population of this country belongs to churches.

Further, the folk-secular celebration of Christmas as a midwinter festival offers satisfactions not found in the Nativity observance. These take the form of holidays from work and school, eating and drinking, traveling, gift acquisition, sociability, and general relaxation from routines. Such attributes of the folk celebration are psychologically attractive and compare favorably with those of the religious observance. Thus it is hardly surprising that the popular phase of the festival now threatens its religious character.

In the main, conflict between the sacred and secular elements in the American Christmas indicates its vigor. Because festivals contain varied beliefs, customs, and symbols, a variety of persons are enabled to answer many different needs and desires. Accordingly, occasions such as Christmas will appeal to the public only so long as both religious and folk interests find ready outlet. Strict ecclesiastical domination of the festival, with suppression of the folk phase, would lead to surreptitious celebration and rebellion. On the other hand, the complete dominance of the folk Christmas, promoted by an excess of commercial zeal, would reduce it to an orgy of gift exchanging, merriment, and sensory gratification. This would eventually eliminate the Christian and fraternal values of the festival. Therefore it appears that a balance between sacred and secular phases of the celebration will enhance its social importance and contribute to its survival.

The Family

Family celebrations of Christmas tend to preserve both aspects of the festival. At the same time they strengthen the ties of kinship. The importance of relatives at Christmas is apparent in the recurring newspaper and magazine accounts of seasonal family reunions, the great increase in travel just before December 25th, the astronomical number of holiday telephone calls, and in the great volume of Christmas mail. A large portion of these activities involves the kinship group. The possible return of the President to his "home" at Christmas is a matter of interest each year. Frequent editorials reinforce the common belief that everyone should be "at home for Christmas" if possible.

During World War II newspapers exhibited pictures of soldiers, taken during the holidays, and displayed marked sympathy for those unable to return home for Christmas. The imputed plight of this group was expressed in a headline, "State Man Flying Coal to Berlin Misses Third Christmas at Home." [15] The pull of the holiday was so great for an American ex-soldier that he swam ashore from a ship at Plymouth, England, to spend Christmas with his English wife and young daughter.[16] In December, 1945, a well known American magazine described how an average Midwestern small-town family spent "Christmas at home." [17] The activities of the parents, their seven children and their wives, husbands, and children were set forth in considerable detail as they prepared Christmas dinner, decorated the tree, sang carols, and distributed presents.

Just before Christmas in 1948, a judge in a New York City court released a husband whose wife had tried to bail him out with money saved from a meager food allowance. The couple wept as they said, "No matter what happens, we'll be together for Christmas." [18]

In an interview in 1951, the wife of Robert Vogeler, an American imprisoned in 1949 by the Communist regime in Hungary, expressed poignantly the feelings of her family about Christmas:

They [two sons] have been taking special care of the Christmas presents they received that terrible December of 1949 so they can show them to their Daddy when he returns to us even if they have to wait the full fifteen years to which the Hungarian Communists sentenced him.[19]

The Vogeler sons' insistence on preserving Christmas presents until their father could see them meant that a "Christmas" had not been missed and that the Vogeler family was psychologically intact in the face of tragedy.

One suspects that the American emphasis on family celebration of Christmas not only is proof of the strength of this group but also reflects fear of its dissolution.[20] The search for jobs takes unnumbered thousands from their homes each year, and many occupations require sacrifice of some aspects of family life. This has resulted in the breakup of numerous families which, nevertheless, use occasions such as Christmas to restore symbolically their lost sense of unity. Where an actual return home at Christmas is not possible, compensatory, "long distance" solidarity is encouraged through gifts and messages.[21] Even those who usually pay little attention to kinship ties are inclined to make some gesture recognizing family membership at Christmas. Thus, this occasion not only leads millions of families to assert and celebrate their existence as small, intimate groups but also increases their awareness of distant kinship ties.

This does not occur by chance, but reflects congruence between the cultural character of the festival and emotional ties of the family. Among the several folk festivals of the year, Christmas alone provides a body of traditional imagery that is family centered. Both the Nativity account and the folk tale of the visit of the gift bringer symbolize important aspects of family life. This is not true of the other holidays, such as New Year's Day, Thanksgiving, Easter, or July 4th, which mark important religious, national, or festive occasions but lack a familial orientation. There is some visiting between families on these holidays, but it misses the significance of "going home for Christmas."

The American family celebration of Christmas is also carried out in a ritual manner. Family holiday activities tend to be repeated each year in about the same fashion. Deviations are frowned upon. These rituals tend to be compulsive so that family members usually act out their parts in the domestic drama, whether agreeable or not. Fixed procedures develop about such matters as the acquisition and decoration of a tree, opening of presents, family singing, and seating arrangements at the dinner. The role appropriate for each person is usually defined by past Christmas experiences.

The following account indicates the unplanned, yet orderly, character of a domestic celebration:

Christmas Eve is always spent in trimming the tree and afterwards going downtown for the mid-night services. Immediately after supper, the balls, tinsel and other ornaments are brought down from the attic while my father is bringing the tree in from outside and setting it in the stand. From then on it is my mother's show. She has to decide where each bauble is to be placed or else she wouldn't think it was just right. On Christmas Day . . . at two or three, our relatives would begin to arrive for the big Christmas Dinner always held at our house. . . . During the visit it is customary for my father to mention six or seven times how much his wife's relatives eat, how much money it costs him. No matter how often repeated, it continually raises a guffaw from my uncle, a sly grin from my aunt and chuckles from the rest.[22]

Minor rituals appear here in nice detail, even to the husband's annual expression of hostility toward his wife's family. The pattern of gift distribution also shows ceremonial characteristics. Thus:

[Christmas Eve] Then comes the moment of the "first gifts." Dad goes to the tree and selects one package to open that evening. He opens it and after it has been duly admired, Mother takes her turn, then I; since my marriage, my husband follows me. Christmas Day, we all return to the tree and, following the order of the night before, we open presents.[23]

The above accounts of domestic celebrations and numerous informal observations point to the existence of a national pattern of family Christmas behavior. It includes conventional activities—such as tree decorating and gift distribution —but allows each family to elaborate and enforce these customs as it sees fit. This pattern also permits variations in the celebrations of groups with diverse ethnic and religious backgrounds.[24] The American pattern of family Christmas behavior is thus a flexible one through which each domestic group marks an important public occasion, but does so in a manner befitting its own needs and preferences.

The fact that some aspects of family Christmas celebrations are ritual in nature means that they are prescribed, are repeated year after year in the same form, and are symbolic. Ritual behavior "stands for" some idea, feeling, value, or experience shared by a given group. Families are prone to use these symbolic acts to express the interrelations of their members, their traditions and collective experiences. For example, in the above description of the distribution of Christmas presents, the manner in which family members select presents constitutes a rite for this group. There is a regular, prescribed order of selecting presents, which begins with the father, passes to the mother, then to the daughter, and finally to the son-in-law, who is a recent addition to the intimate group. Each person's role in the ceremony of gift selection apparently symbolizes his position in the family. The other examples illustrate the use of domestic rites to preserve memories of previous Christmas celebrations and to recognize the roles of different members. This usually promotes continuity between generations and contributes unity to the kinship group.

In spite of the conserving influence of ritual, the domestic Christmas celebration must be adapted to basic changes in family structure. One source of these is marriage, which raises the issue of where and how new couples will celebrate Christmas. This indicates that the occasion has special significance for the newly wed and their families. Solutions of this problem are affected by the residence of the couple in relation to that of their parents, the strength of family ties, the husband's occupation, and past significance of the celebration. Newly married couples often alternate early Christmas celebrations between the home of the wife and that of the husband, or spend Thanksgiving with one family and Christmas with the other. Some divide Christmas Eve and Christmas Day between the two.

With the appearance of children, there is a tendency to hold celebrations at the home of the grandparents until the children are five or six years old. Around this time the more recent parents and young children begin to celebrate Christmas in their own home and invite the grandparents to join them. This suggests a shift in dominance within the original kinship group. An interesting study by Sussman showed that in those instances where the children married in a manner approved by their parents, their families had observed Christmas in a traditional fashion.[25] He found convincing evidence that Christmas rituals both expressed and promoted continuity between generations of a family.

Within the family, Christmas gifts symbolize not only seasonal generosity but also the inner life of the group. This is especially true of children, who often interpret their position in the family in terms of their gifts. Painful childhood experiences involving Christmas gifts tend to persist throughout adult life, as illustrated by Lincoln Steffens's account of a "Miserable Merry Christmas":

I saw that my stocking was empty; it hung limp; not a thing in it; and under and around it—nothing. . . . I can feel now what I felt then, and I am sure that if one could see the wounds upon our hearts, there will be found still upon mine a scar from that terrible Christmas.[26]

Christmas presents are often involved in the emotional problems of children. This is especially true of difficulties which involve their parents and siblings. A Negro, describing his childhood emotional struggles, asserted that gifts at a particular Christmas had disillusioned him keenly and crystallized a conviction which he carried into adult life:

The longing for tenderness from his parents . . . accumulated on a particular Christmas in his fifth year. He had desperately expected some mark of preferment in the type of Christmas presents which he would receive. . . . Christmas morning came, and the presents were just ordinary presents, not much better than those of the other children; perhaps not as good in some ways. . . . All right, then, it was every man for himself, and one got affection wherever one could get it and expected nothing more for nothing.[27]

Parents' efforts to create an atmosphere of make-believe and excitement for the children at Christmas suggest their own involvement in the holiday euphoria. Some attempt to reproduce the pleasures of their own childhood. Others are determined that their children shall enjoy Christmas in a manner denied them. Each family's celebration is also influenced by prevailing neighborhood customs. Children are effective agents for enforcing conformity because most parents are uncomfortable when reproached with "The other children have it at their house" or "Why can't we do what everybody else does?" This is probably the source of the greatest pressure on Jewish families to adopt the "gentile Christmas."

The folk celebration is centered in the family and is largely controlled by women. Though this does not accord with their power position in American society, it may reflect their special functions at Christmas. That is, women buy and prepare most of the gifts for the occasion as well as provide holiday food and delicacies. This liberality generates physical and psychological gratification which is bound to enhance their importance in the festival. In addition, women somehow symbolize the kinship and humanitarian values traditionally associated with Christmas. Perhaps they are permitted and encouraged to dominate our most important national festival as symbolic compensation for accepting the disadvantages of their social role.

Like other festivals, Christmas is followed by a sense of "letdown," which succeeds periods of intense preparation and participation in a celebration. Post-Christmas cartoons portray the average father wondering how he will manage to pay the accumulated Christmas bills, and "letters to the editor" deplore the "secularization" of the festival and the extravagance of holiday gifts. Husbands are supposed to wear reluctantly the ties given them by female relatives, and wives rush to department stores to exchange presents. Children bandy questions on the theme of "What did you get for Christmas?" and invidious boasting is expected. W. H. Auden has described tellingly the domestic aftermath of the American Christmas in middle-class homes:

Well, so that is that. Now we must dismantle the tree,
Putting the decorations back into their cardboard boxes—
Some have got broken—and carrying them up to the attic.
The holly and the mistletoe must be taken down and burnt,
And the children got ready for school. There are enough
Left-overs to do, warmed up, for the rest of the week—
Not that we have much appetite, having drunk such a lot,
Stayed up so late, attempted—quite unsuccessfully—
To love all of our relatives and, in general
Grossly overestimated our powers.[28]

It remains to say that Christmas not only affects the family unit internally but also relates it to the larger society and culture. Thus, the Christmas festival provides an opportunity for each family to participate in an important national festival even though it does so in a private celebration. This promotes family-community integration, yet preserves the uniqueness of each family group.

The School

The Christmas celebration occupies an important place in the American public school as well as in the church and the family. This is evident in the national custom of the Christmas school vacation and preholiday observances. School vacations at midwinter festivals are very old and can be traced back to pre-Christian Rome. Nevertheless, custom permitted only a one-day Christmas vacation from school at Salem, Massachusetts, as late as 1818.[29] However, as the popularity of the celebration increased during the post Civil War period, laws were enacted by the various states making Christmas Day a legal holiday for public schools. This legislation was not common until the 1890 decade, though a few states enacted laws of this type somewhat earlier.[30]

By 1931 forty-one states had laws requiring the dismissal of public schools on December 25th.[31] This day outranks any other occasion—such as Thanksgiving or Washington's Birthday—as judged by the number of states in which it is a legal holiday. Furthermore, local custom sanctions a school holiday on Christmas Day in some states even though this is not established by legislative action. In addition to the legal holiday on December 25th, most schools close for a longer vacation period during the Christmas season. The length of the school holiday is set either by regulations of the state boards of education or by local school boards.

Legislators have defined Christmas Day as a legal holiday, but teachers have evinced most interest in pre-Christmas school programs as a means of helping students develop understanding of the occasion. They have sought to achieve this through classroom and assembly programs. These usually involve display of the tree, carol and hymn singing, reading of Christmas classics, classroom parties, exchange of presents, and gifts to the needy. In some public schools plays dealing with the life of Jesus have been included in the pre-Christmas exercises. Two recent studies indicate that such programs are common in all parts of the United States.[32]

These activities reflect the fact that both Christmas and the schools are chiefly concerned with the young. In view of the "youth" orientation of American culture, it would be strange if those agencies devoted to training youth ignored a festival in which children have so prominent a place. In addition, the school observance of a community festival indicates integration between these important social units.

Certain problems have arisen in connection with school-room pre-Christmas observances. This is especially true of gift giving, carol singing, and Nativity plays. In schoolrooms where students have been permitted and encouraged to give Christmas presents to classmates, some have received numerous presents and others none, with consequent dissatisfaction. Teachers have resorted to devices such as "drawing names" to eliminate the unequal distribution of presents. Under this system every member of a class draws the name of one classmate, so that each student receives only one present and the selection is left to chance. This has proved a fairly satisfactory solution of a situation which otherwise might nullify the teachings of brotherhood and generosity long associated with the occasion. It also demonstrates the importance of equalitarianism in American culture.

Another problem which has plagued teachers concerns accepting Christmas gifts from their students. In some instances presents have been valuable enough to suggest bribery. In other cases students unable to afford Christmas presents for their teachers have felt unhappily conspicuous. These complications have led some boards of education to forbid their teachers accepting any Christmas presents from their students.

By far the most serious problem associated with public school observance of Christmas arises from the fact that these activities involve the introduction of religious elements such as carol singing and Nativity plays into a secular school system.[33] Jewish rabbis and parents often insist that these pre-Christmas activities violate their religious rights. Protests have been made since the beginning of the present century, and show no sign of abating. Many Christians and some Jews maintain that the pre-Christmas programs of the public schools are chiefly secular, and emphasize folk rather than religious aspects of the occasion. Jewish leaders reject this interpretation and point out that the core of Christmas is the Nativity, even though pagan and folk customs constitute part of the seasonal celebration. The Rabbinical Assembly of America asserted in 1946:

Christmas may have many general folk elements which are popular with children. But sincere and thoughtful Christians will surely agree that Christmas is primarily a religious festival. . . . The practice of calling on Jewish children to join in the singing of Christmas carols, to take part in Christmas plays . . . must be regarded as an infringement on their rights as Americans.[34]

Other Jewish groups have taken a more moderate stand on this issue, as in the case of the Central Conference of American Rabbis. This group counseled Jewish parents to forbid their children's participation in singing Christmas carols but not to make objections to this practice in public schools.[35]

Jewish parents are often keenly aware of the results of forbidding their children to sing carols in public school and community Christmas programs. A Jewish mother described her conflicts over Christmas observances in an article entitled "Christmas-Chanuka—December Is the Cruelest Month," and said of the Jewish celebration: "Chanuka begins, perhaps, on the day a Jewish child may remark, 'There are two times I hate school most—Christmas and Easter. And I hate Christmas most.' " [36] She continued:

This not having Christmas, when all the world has Christmas was itself a brutality. . . . In America now, this is the worst Judaism can do to a young child. No Christmas. After that, everything Judaism can do is sheer profit. [37]

A number of schools have attempted to bridge the religious gap between Christians and Jews at this season by presenting joint Christmas-Chanuka programs at an assembly. These programs have been carried out chiefly in urban areas and, in several cities, have been presented successfully for a number of years. Schools in Springfield, Massachusetts; Atlantic City, New Jersey; Omaha, Nebraska; Detroit, Michigan; Seattle, Washington, and other places have continued joint celebrations, apparently satisfied with the results or unwilling to relinquish the practice. [38] Neither among Christians nor among Jews is there unanimity as to the value of the joint celebrations, though the latter group, as a minority, has more at stake in continuing them than does the larger Christian element.

Christmas observance in the public schools is accepted without question by most Christians, and a direct challenge to the legitimacy of the practice appears absurd to many. However, Jews are on strong logical ground in objecting to such ceremonies in public schools because there is no doubt that even the folk attributes of Christmas are embedded in a matrix of beliefs and customs related to Christianity. Furthermore, some of the folk symbols have acquired a semireligious meaning through long association with Nativity accounts. Thus, the Christmas tree, though originally derived from pagan midwinter festivals, has acquired overtones of Christian significance, even though it did not appear in the Nativity story.

It is interesting that schools continue to observe Christmas with vacations, special exercises, gifts, and parties in spite of the difficulties this involves. There is little in the culture of the school that is directly relevant to the traditions, imagery, and sentiments either of the religious or of the folk aspects of the occasion. Children constitute the only element prominent in both the school room and the annual festival. In addition, the Christmas vacation is an awkward interruption of classroom activity and requires considerable adjustment of educational procedures. Nevertheless, school vacations at Christmas are customary at all educational levels and required by law in some instances.

One suspects that the schools of this country observe Christmas chiefly because of indirect community pressure. Thus, if schools ignored Christmas, it would be very difficult to maintain discipline and attention in the classroom if other agencies, such as the family, church, clubs, and stores, were preparing to celebrate the occasion. Therefore, by accepting the celebration and making necessary adjustments to it, the school has been able to adapt Christmas to its educational and administrative program. This enables teachers partly to control the amount of time and attention devoted to the celebration in the classroom. It also affords them an opportunity to inculcate important values such as brotherhood, generosity, and kindness under favorable circumstances inasmuch as these are strongly supported by the communal spirit of Christmas. This promotes integration of school and community values and helps to perpetuate the festival.

Bounty and Beneficence

In addition to the participation of churches, families, and schools in Christmas, another important aspect of the celebration is found in the charitable activity it engenders. This comes about both through organized welfare agencies and through countless acts of beneficence by individuals. It is nurtured by a belief in the ideals of charity, generosity, and kindness.

These ideals are intimately connected with both religious and secular aspects of the occasion, and they exhibit an obligatory character at Christmas which reflects the special circumstances of their American development. In nineteenth century United States the charitable sentiments long associated with Christmas were nurtured by a general climate of humanitarianism. For example, a New York City magazine editorialized just before Christmas in 1842:

We should remember, while enjoying the festivities of the day, that to the poor, Christmas brings but few pleasures unless some thoughtful neighbor for one day in the year spreads their humble board for them.[39]

While the seventeenth and eighteenth century Christmas celebrations had included generosity to the poor, those of the nineteenth century gave greatly increased emphasis to this precept.

It is interesting to recall that some Protestant denominations long opposed the religious celebration of Christmas and that their leaders yielded reluctantly to the popular demand for the festival.[40] Notwithstanding this fact, Christian teachings of brotherhood and generosity constituted the main source of nineteenth century humanitarianism, and most of its proponents were church members. As Christmas became a popular folk festival about the middle of the last century, it drew upon the resources of both secular humanitarianism and the traditional beneficence of Christianity. Before the days of organized welfare agencies and modern social security, Christmas offered a fitting occasion for the informal expression of brotherhood and kindness, particularly to the poor, the unfortunate, and the unhappy. Furthermore, the increasing wealth of the United States in the period after the Civil War may have promoted a greater sense of the possibility, as well as of the obligation, of active charity.[41]

Two general types of liberality and sympathy for the unfortunate are manifested in the American Christmas: the informal, individualized kind, and organized activities, planned and carried out by groups and formal agencies. Newspaper accounts describe many spontaneous acts of Christmas charity and thoughtfulness directed both at children and at adults. The greatest concern is manifested for the young who are not expected to live until Christmas or for those fatally ill at the holiday time. Headlines suggest the intensity of public response to news about such unfortunate children: "Mother's Appeal Brings 10,000 Cards, TV Set and Gifts to Bed-Ridden Girl"; "Hymn Record Comforts Dying Girl Celebrating Early Christmas"; "Children Share Christmas Party with Sick Girl." [42]

Continued interest in the critically ill child who has survived to celebrate Christmas in spite of medical predictions was revealed in the story "Youngster Has Third 'Borrowed' Christmas." [43] Arrangements are made frequently for a Santa Claus to visit children who must remain in a hospital at Christmas. A six-year-old girl whose family was killed in a fire just before Christmas became the beneficiary of a trust fund quickly established by public subscription to provide for her care and education. A report said, "Strangers brought gifts for her and went away without leaving their names." [44] Such anonymous generosity demonstrates a deep sympathy for orphaned children, which finds an almost compulsive expression at Christmas.

Adults who suffer great misfortune near Christmas also receive generous assistance, as was demonstrated in the case of a New Hampshire family whose house was destroyed by fire a few days before the holiday. Food, clothing, and temporary shelter were supplied by friends, neighbors, and strangers. They also bought a Christmas tree and presents for the children. The wife and mother of the family declared, "I never saw anything like it in my life, the way people are joining in and helping." [45] Undoubtedly there is also much individual alleviation of economic distress at Christmas, but since such acts are not recorded little is known of their extent and character.

For numerous organizations, Christmas is an annual occasion for liberality on a scale not attained at any other time of the year. Local welfare agencies, churches, the Red Cross, Salvation Army, service clubs, the Tuberculosis Association, American Legion, Veterans of Foreign Wars, and others collect funds for charity in advance of Christmas and provide these tangible evidences of kindness and generosity to many who would otherwise be neglected at Christmas time. Each year those in institutions and hospitals receive special attention at the holidays, and parties for "underprivileged" children are given in cities and towns throughout the country. Men's service clubs are particularly active in this type of charity, and prisons, jails, mental institutions, sanatoria, and convalescent homes reflect the festive and humanitarian sentiments of the season.

Christmas charity is often duplicated, occasionally with unfortunate consequences. This is evident in a letter from a patient in a Midwestern hospital:

Christmas here at the Pest House was quite a thing. Never before have I seen it observed so enthusiastically. Brass bands, girl scout carollers, and string trios paraded through the halls for ten days prior to Christmas. Being an ex-G.I., I was visited and showered by the American Legion (both male and female branches), Forty & Eighters, American War Mothers and others. It became progressively more embarrassing until I finally put my foot down when the Salvation Army tried to bless me with some fruit and candy. Needless to say, the "take" was pretty terrific and I'm sure the strain of the holiday season didn't put many of us back more than a month in our progress toward recovery.[46]

Social work agencies have found that the orgy of Christmas generosity sometimes upsets long-run plans for their clients and brings results that are professionally undesirable. A case worker wrote:

Few agency workers ever pass through the pre-Christmas season without headaches. . . . Frequently the headache is intensified by the feeling that the results of weary hours of interpretation to both client and the community, over the rest of the year, are blotted out by an orgy of misdirected giving at Christmas.[47]

One agency, concerned with a special type of case work, decided to refuse Christmas gifts which were inconsistent with its objectives and methods. By making careful explanations to generous donors, it was able to control and use professionally the flow of Christmas gifts to its clients.

The *New York Times* began a special type of Christmas appeal in 1912 to raise money from December to March each year to aid unusually deserving people in distress. This campaign, known as the "100 Neediest Cases," began in 1912 with 117 gifts amounting to $3,600, and rose to over 14,000 gifts totaling about $400,000 by 1946. For several Sundays before Christmas, the *Times* describes a number of the neediest cases. The reliability of information on each case is verified by a professional social work agency. This is done to avoid duplication of effort and to assure the donors that their money is well used. Contributions to this appeal are received from individuals and groups as diversified as bridge clubs and employees of foreign embassies at Washington, D.C. One family sent a donation to this fund and wrote:

The thought of the NEEDIEST is as much a part of our Christmas as carols and sleighbells. It comes to our family with dinner, warmth of baking pies, children's laughter, crackling tissue paper and shouts of "Merry Christmas." [48]

Christmas charity occasionally resembles one aspect of the Roman Saturnalia, when master and slave exchanged places. At a dinner given to 1,500 hoboes by the St. Louis House of Delegates in 1913, aldermen served as waiters and bus boys, and city officials donated to support the dinner. When a preacher talked overlong, after the dinner, one old tramp interrupted with, "Cut out the Christmas cheer talk and give us more coffee." [49]

Amnesty to those in jail or prison is still practiced at Christmas, and the holiday is often made the occasion for granting pardons or for commuting sentences. General Douglas MacArthur granted a Christmas amnesty to Japanese war leaders in December, 1949.[50] This act of official clemency is particularly interesting because Christmas is not a Japanese holiday and would presumably have significance only for those nationals who had become Christians. It is doubtful that this was true of all the prisoners released on this occasion. One can only speculate on the reasons for this act.

A final example of the tortuous ways of Christmas kindness appears in the strenuous efforts made by Connecticut officials to deliver unemployment compensation checks before Christmas in 1949. State employees worked overtime and postal authorities gave the checks special handling to assure delivery before the holiday. A newspaper report was given the interesting headline, "Checks Speeded to Jobless in Time for Yule Shopping." [51]

Christmas kindness and bounty even include animals. State societies for the prevention of cruelty to animals and branches of the Animal Rescue League often provide food and blankets for horses at Christmas. In Detroit, Michigan, the local Humane Society has held an annual party for horses for the past twenty years, at which time each horse is given a large stocking containing hay, oats, carrots, apples, and several lumps of sugar. As one member of the society explained, "After all, horses have feelings too." [52] Department stores report an increase in the sale of gifts for dogs and cats at Christmas. This may reflect ancient folk beliefs about the presence of animals in the Nativity scene or, more likely, the fact that domestic pets are symbolically members of families and consequently share in Christmas generosity.

A note of grim irony was introduced into the Christmas of December, 1944, by the *New Yorker*, which reminded Americans of the "Christmas" gifts received that year from our armed forces, such as Eniwetok, Los Negros Islands, Castelforte, and Saint-Lô. These were captured at bloody cost, and the magazine concluded its acknowledgment of the tragic bounty: "There isn't time to look at them all. It will take years. This is a Christmas you will never forget, people have been *so generous*." [53]

The annual outpouring of generosity and good will at Christmas raises the interesting question, Why does this happen? It is, of course, possible that Christmas is simply an occasion, hallowed by tradition, which prescribes fraternal and benevolent deeds. This explanation is hardly convincing. It does not account for the sense of urgency which characterizes Christmas kindness and good works. At this time the expression of good will has a compulsive quality not appearing at other times of the year. This is manifested concretely in the lavish gifts which strangers send to sick children and in the irrational duplication of presents which formal organizations give to those in hospitals and welfare institutions. It even extends the "spirit" of the season to animals and often produces bizarre examples of kindness, as in the Christmas parties for horses.

A more tenable explanation of the forces underlying Christmas charity is possible if it is viewed in relation to prevailing social values. For instance, brotherhood is one of our accepted moral ideals, yet is frequently neglected in daily life. Undoubtedly this causes feelings of guilt and uneasiness in many persons and leads some to try to banish them by acts of charity that are often irrational. Thus, paradoxically, Christmas beneficence draws support both from traditional values and from the contradictions of contemporary life.

This interpretation also raises the question of why Americans slight accepted beliefs in brotherhood and cooperation. One answer is that our society indoctrinates its members with the belief that each individual ought to attain some tangible form of success, preferably through competition. This point of view prevails in business, politics, education, sports and, to a degree, family life, as well as in charitable giving. In so far as Americans have imbibed this heady drink of socially induced ambition, they tend to ignore or slight the precepts of brotherhood, kindness, and cooperation in favor of those related to attaining individual success. However, many persons experience a sharp conflict of values because, though the ideals of brotherhood and kindness are relegated to a secondary place, they retain their normative quality. Therefore widespread feelings of guilt develop from this clash of divergent social norms and furnish some of the motivation for Christmas charity.

In addition, sentiments of brotherhood and charity are not completely suppressed by the dominance of success goals and the exigencies of competition. Generous public support of a variety of welfare agencies is proof of this. However, charitable activity is increasingly carried on by rational means and through formal organizations. This reduces the satisfactions which might develop through the immediate, personal contact of donor and recipient and undoubtedly leaves many persons with an unfulfilled desire to help the needy in a more direct manner. Christmas offers an opportunity to gain this type of satisfaction and produces countless acts of individual charity and kindness, as well as substantial contributions to welfare agencies.

It should be said in passing that the mass media of communication have stimulated both individual and organizational types of holiday charity. This is especially true of newspapers, which carry details of the plight of the needy at Christmas and dramatize them in stories and pictures. As a consequence, strangers frequently offer assistance to persons they know of only through news accounts.

In perspective, it seems clear that American churches, families, schools, and charitable agencies celebrate Christmas according to a common pattern, yet emphasize those aspects of the festival which foster their special interests. In addition, the Christmas activities of such groups constitute the core of the celebration and tend to preserve and strengthen both its religious and its humanitarian values. At the same time, these groups are invigorated by participating in a communal festival which reduces social distinctions and overleaps the bounds of convention. This rewarding experience promises perpetuation of the festival for a long time to come and suggests that secularization of the occasion does not necessitate loss of its social vitality.

At this point it remains to examine the way in which commercial exploitation has affected Christmas both in its religious and in its secular aspects. This will make possible a fuller understanding of the impact of secular forces on the celebration.

CHAPTER IV.

Exploiting a Festival

The growing importance of Christmas in the American economy reflects chiefly the increasing efforts of commercial interests to exploit its traditions and sentiments for profit. This is especially apparent in retail business, although the demand for holiday goods also affects wholesale trade and manufacturing. Merchants began holiday advertising as early as the 1830's and, by the 1890 decade, business influences in the celebration were numerous.[1] However, the studied exploitation of the festival did not develop fully until the third decade of the present century.

This came about as an indirect result of the abnormal demands made on industry and commerce by World War I, which caused large-scale expansion both of the productive and of the distributive facilities of the nation. At the close of the war in 1918, the American economy was geared to a high level of output, and a host of new products were ready to be sold.[2] However, consumer demand was shrinking, and there was serious danger of a stagnant market.

In this dilemma business leaders sought some means of increasing normal, peacetime buying, and turned to promotion and high-pressure sales methods. Both merchants and advertising agencies recognized the commercial potentialities of folk festivals, and began to exploit these occasions shortly after 1920. This was immediately successful and has continued unabated to the present.

The Christmas-Gift Custom

From a commercial standpoint the usefulness of Christmas depends on the extent to which people give presents. If the practice is followed by most persons, it affords a regular annual demand for certain types of goods. It also provides businessmen with some information on the nature and extent of seasonal wants from year to year. Because our giving conventions are amenable to suggestion and direction through advertising, merchants have tried to maximize the public's sense of both the propriety and the obligation of giving presents at Christmas. In addition, they have not been reluctant to suggest the types of gifts appropriate both to persons and to the occasion.

The association of presents with Christmas is not an old one, and the contemporary emphasis on holiday gifts did not develop until the nineteenth century. In European countries children had long received nuts, candies, oranges, and cakes on St. Nicholas's day. These were reputedly brought by such figures as St. Nicholas, Kris Kindlein, or Knecht Rupprecht. Parents often added a doll or a toy to the bounty of the gift bringers. However, the American colonists did not consider presents for adults very important during the seventeenth and eighteenth centuries. They recognized an old obligation of Christmas charity to the needy, and the wealthy contributed something for the holiday cheer of the working classes and the poor. However, during the nineteenth century the Christmas-gift custom spread to all areas and groups in the United States. It became an accepted seasonal convention observed by adults and children alike.

Today the annual flow of Christmas gifts occurs chiefly between social equals and informally defines the relationship of donors and recipients. Most of this giving takes place between family members, friends, those romantically involved, neighbors, and business associates.[3] The greatest holiday expenditures are made for such things as jewelry, apparel, toys, books, and toilet goods. Millions of Americans annually exchange these presents, and a great deal of their holiday giving is expected to be reciprocal, that is, the donor gives to those from whom he expects to receive presents. Folk humor has characterized this yearly exchange as the "Big Swap."

In spite of its acquisitive, materialistic character, the annual traffic is affected by the ties of kinship, by friendship, and other social values. Particularly in families, it reflects the degree of intimacy, age, sex, and the comparative affluence of those involved. These factors also mute the demand for reciprocity in Christmas giving. For example, young children look forward to Christmas gifts from their parents without feeling a sense of mutual obligation. However, siblings of approximately equal years expect presents from each other, as do husbands and wives. The aged and infirm of reduced circumstances may anticipate Christmas gifts from younger or more affluent kin without requirement of a return gift. Outside the immediate family, there is no consensus defining the gift obligations of relatives. Each family devises its rules in light of its traditions, closeness, and individual preferences.

Outside the kinship group, little is known of the nature of Christmas giving. Informal observation suggests that women exchange presents more frequently than do men. The single woman often makes gifts to the children of her married friends, though bachelors are less likely to do so. Childless married couples may send such holiday presents, but usually end this practice when the children reach adolescence. Varied motives prompt these acts of generosity. For the most part, Christmas gifts simply express the significance of the relation to the donor.

Sweethearts may exchange presents, though the initiative is supposed to lie with the male. Humorous comment suggests that males often arrange a timely end to a romantic relation which might obligate them at Christmas. The character of gifts exchanged by those "in love" or "going together" or "engaged" will vary with age and social class, as well as with individual preferences.

In the main, Christmas giving demonstrates the countless efforts to fulfill important social obligations. Thus, annually, millions of persons consider which relatives, friends, and associates they are obligated to by social ties or as the donors of previous gifts. In addition, gifts are supposed to express personal affection and regard. This means that Christmas presents should symbolize the social relations of those involved as well as express the personal feelings of the donor.

Failure to observe these conventions may be interpreted as evidence that a person is a "Scrooge"—a severe indictment— or that he is unable to play his social role for financial reasons or lack of taste. This causes many persons to dread the annual "Big Swap" lest they omit names from their list, or shop unwisely. To assist them, and to promote sales, many department stores provide special personnel to advise customers in their selections.

An interesting feature of Christmas giving is the informal but stringent demand that presents be wrapped and addressed. Convention requires that they be prepared, at least in a token manner, before presentation. This item of usage underscores the fact that a "gift" expresses personal regard and also symbolizes the social relations of donor and recipient. Insistence on the correct preparation of gifts has created a sizable demand for special paper, colored twine, ribbon, and cards. It has even brought into existence a commercial practice termed "gift wrapping."

Interestingly, this activity falls chiefly within the woman's sphere. In most homes she is responsible for wrapping the

Christmas presents, except for those she will receive. In stores, women clerks usually wrap gifts for males, who are not expected to possess this skill. This woman's cult includes tying special knots and bows on packages, matching the ribbon, paper, and so on. When presents are opened, the recipient is expected to appreciate the attractiveness of the package. Women who wrap presents skillfully receive a modicum of recognition for their ability.

The conventions which concern the preparation of Christmas presents extend even to money or checks. These gifts are presented usually in an envelope with the recipient's name indicated. There is a fairly general preference for money gifts to consist of unused currency. Some persons even consider it improper and insulting to present an unwrapped or unprepared Christmas gift. Those who offer unwrapped gifts usually comment on the omission, and thus indirectly offer an apology.

The reciprocal emphasis in Christmas giving has spawned the half serious, half comic notion of retaliatory giving. This practice involves sending an undesirable present to someone who has previously given the donor a dubious one. Potter discussed this with malicious humor in an article entitled "Christmas-ship, or the Art of Giving and Receiving." [4] He asserted that the purpose of calculated Christmas giving is:

1. To make it seem to everybody present that the receiver is getting something better than he has given you.
2. To make the receiver feel that you have got away with a present that looks all right but which he knows really is not.
3. To make the receiver feel that there is some implied criticism about the present you have chosen.

The incidence of this type of Christmas giving is probably slight, but warrants wry comment and amused appreciation of Potter's article. The theme also appears in "popular" Christmas plays.[5]

Contemporary Christmas usage also includes one or two types of pseudo-giving. For example, the urban practice of giving holiday "presents" to postmen, policemen, janitors, elevator men, and so on, is mostly a form of insurance against bad service in the future rather than an expression of seasonal good will or generosity. The business world is plagued, also, by the practice of using Christmas "presents" as a polite form of bribery or tribute. Many firms condemn this, and forbid their employees to accept such "gifts." However, in some groups it is necessary to give "Christmas presents" to maintain satisfactory commercial relations. Obviously, this is not an example of the traditional generosity.

Thus, Christmas giving has a complex character. In some instances it is a means of expressing important sentiments of social and personal regard, while in others the custom is used to pursue utilitarian ends having little to do with the traditional occasion. In spite of some abuse it is firmly rooted in contemporary American life, and provides the element which is both necessary and sufficient to exploit Christmas successfully. Business firms make plans for their "holiday" trade each year, secure in the knowledge that most Americans will both want and feel obliged to give Christmas presents to one another.

"Promoting" Christmas

Commercial exploitation of Christmas in the United States has been systematic and thorough. American business and financial groups have not only stimulated wants through extensive advertising and publicity but have also provided agencies which encourage millions of persons to save money for buying Christmas gifts each year. One of these is an organization termed the "Christmas Club," which came into existence in 1910 and had over 10 million members by 1950.

During that year the members deposited over 950 million dollars in thousands of Christmas Clubs throughout the United States. This means of saving is available in about 6,200 banks located in every state in the country.[6]

A survey of Christmas Club members in 1950 indicated that they planned to use about 38 per cent of their current savings to buy Christmas presents.[7] This amounted to more than 365 million dollars made available in that year through the agency of Christmas Clubs. One cannot fail to be struck by the fact that interest in buying Christmas gifts has influenced millions of persons to save money systematically for fifty weeks each year before the annual festival. The amount of savings is also a tribute to the sagacity of financial organizations which have provided an effective means of exploiting sentiments basic to the holiday.

Business promotion in the form of advertising, decorations, music, and community parades has become the inevitable precursor of each Christmas. This is borne out by informal observation and by the increase in newspaper display advertising during November and December.[8]

Figures on recent newspaper advertising indicate a sharp monthly rise, which begins in October, mounts to a peak in December, then falls sharply during January and February. The increase between November and December is much greater than that between October and November, indicating intensified promotion as Christmas approaches. Magazine advertising is used also to stimulate holiday buying, though the peak of these efforts is reached in November, rather than in December. To date, radio and television publicity for the holiday season has not been used as extensively as have the printed word and pictures.

Christmas advertising seeks to attract attention and stimulate desires for goods by associating them with well known holiday symbols. This entails the seasonal use of representations of the folk celebration such as Santa Claus and his reindeer-drawn sleigh, the Christmas tree, holly, ivy, mistletoe, green boughs, lighted candles, bells, stars, and carolers. In addition, pictures of snow-covered landscapes, especially those of open country, are often used, as well as scenes portraying the traditional English Christmas. In recent years Rudolph the Red-Nosed Reindeer has been included as an established figure of the folk festival, though usually in association with Santa Claus. Deer, squirrels, rabbits, and birds also appear in display advertising. Occasionally, commercial groups use scenes from the Nativity tale, but this is infrequent. Conventional phrases, well worn but serviceable for annual use, accompany representations of the folk celebration. The most frequently used ones are: "The joy of Christmas," "an old-fashioned Christmas," "the spirit of giving," "the spirit of Christmas," and "peace on earth, good will to men." The conventional holiday salutation of "Merry Christmas and a Happy New Year" appears constantly in advertisements.

Printed Christmas advertisements use most of the "appeals" of non-holiday publicity. Merchants advertise a variety of "appropriate" goods, ranging from cigars to autos, by associating them with holiday symbols. They suggest that their goods will demonstrate seasonal kindness and generosity, or will enhance the prestige and popularity of the donor. Only the sexual and romantic love themes, so common in other advertising, are omitted or given slight attention in Christmas promotion. The historical character of the holiday both aids and hampers advertisers, since it provides them with a convenient body of popular, traditional symbols which, however, resist innovations and permit only limited manipulation.

In numerous communities merchants have established a "Christmas shopping season," which is often opened with some public ceremony. It begins usually on the Monday after Thanksgiving.[9] Newspapers announce that the "City Starts Annual Shopping Spree" to give the period the proper festive flavor. Many towns and cities stage public events, such as parades, to initiate the "season." Local merchants usually arrange and finance such activities, which achieve some slight measure of community feeling, as well as signalize the imminence of the annual festival. Business groups provide trees, green boughs, and colored lights to decorate main streets in thousands of American cities and towns each year. While loudspeakers blare forth carols and popular Christmas songs, advertisements remind readers that there are only so many shopping days until Christmas.

The period of commercial preparation for celebrating Christmas gathers momentum as December 25th approaches, creating a sense of urgency and excitement. Everyone is urged to get his Christmas shopping done early lest he be unable to buy the "correct" gift or cause late delivery of his presents. The mounting intensity of the shopping period has led one writer to characterize it as "a good fight to all."

Effects on Business

Systematic exploitation of traditional Christmas generosity and of the gift-exchanging custom is effective in increasing retail business during the holiday season. This can be seen by comparing December retail sales figures with those of adjacent months. Table II below indicates the amount of money spent for all types of retail goods by months during

TABLE II. MONTHLY VARIATIONS IN ALL TYPES OF RETAIL SALES IN THE UNITED STATES 1946–1952 [10]

MILLIONS OF DOLLARS

Year	Sept.	Oct.	Nov.	Dec.	Jan.	Feb.
1946–47	8,698	9,432	9,556	10,847	8,299	7,876
1947–48	10,252	10,941	10,672	12,641	9,684	8,948
1948–49	11,058	11,542	11,019	13,194	9,416	8,918
1949–50	10,998	11,125	10,872	12,846	9,522	9,281
1950–51	12,498	12,077	11,613	14,463	12,155	11,167
1951–52	12,410	13,190	12,702	14,632	11,338	11,181

six-month periods from 1946 through 1952. The figures include both durable (hardware, jewelry, and so on) and non-durable (clothing, liquor, and so on) goods. In spite of lumping together both holiday and non-holiday kinds of goods, the over-all increase in December sales indicates the influence of Christmas on purchases.

The table shows a sharp increase in December sales each year throughout the period. Even though the volume grew year by year, there was a noticeable rise in receipts each December, followed by a marked decline during January and February. Because the years covered by Table II came after World War II, and were free from wartime price restrictions, variations in monthly sales can be assumed to express buyers' wishes. Thus it is reasonable to conclude that Christmas buying is responsible for a major part of the December increases.

The impact of Christmas buying on December business is even more apparent if one examines retail sales figures of specific types of merchandise. Some kinds seem to reflect the influence of holiday purchases, while others remain stable or even decline in December. The next table shows some of these variations.

TABLE III.   MONTHLY VARIATIONS IN RETAIL SALES
BY TYPE OF STORE FOR 1950 [11]

RETAIL SALES	PER CENT OF YEAR'S SALES MADE IN DECEMBER [*]
Building materials	7.0
Department stores	14.8
Drugstores	11.0
Eating and drinking places	8.9
Family and other apparel	15.0
General merchandise	14.5
Jewelry	22.7
Liquor	15.0
Men's clothing and furnishings	16.0
Women's apparel and accessories	13.1

[*] If sales were constant, each month would account for approximately 8.3 of the annual total.

Undoubtedly December sales of retail goods reflect the combined influence of several factors. Christmas-gift customs, the onset of winter, changes in fashion and family buying habits—all these exert a concerted influence on December business and push it to the highest point of the year. One suspects that heavy purchases of jewelry, liquor, and toilet articles, as well as some kinds of luxury apparel, reflect primarily the influence of holiday gift customs. Those in modest financial circumstances frequently give clothing and household equipment at Christmas in the effort to add a festive touch to a present of the "necessity" type. It is a tribute to the cultural significance of the occasion that it is able to endow these practical articles with a special seasonal value.

Children's toys also constitute an important aspect of Christmas business, and their manufacture and sale have undergone an interesting development in this country. As late as 1923 the United States imported far more toys, in terms of monetary value, than it exported. At that time toys came chiefly from Czechoslovakia, Germany, and Japan. Since World War II our toy imports have come chiefly from the United Kingdom, though in 1948 the United States resumed this type of trade with Germany and Japan. However, between 1923 and 1947 there was a sharp reversal of position.[12] As of 1948, American manufacturers exported over five times the value of toys imported into this country. This shift in position has come about through increasingly successful competition by American firms.

Toy manufacturers and distributors have undertaken to increase their sales throughout the year, and especially outside the Christmas season. It is estimated that slightly over one-half of the year's retail business in toys is now done during the Christmas season. In 1947 the total value of toy production in the United States was estimated at $322,000,000.[13]

The economic importance of toys in Christmas business is a reflection of their cultural and psychological significance in American society. They are symbols of the children's world, and the annual Christmas traffic in toys demonstrates the social importance of the young and also provides clues to the role of playthings in our culture. American adults seem to acknowledge a "right" of children to receive some kind of gift at Christmas. Thus, parents consider "toys for the children" the first requirement of the domestic celebration, and the numerous organizations which give parties for "underprivileged" children always include playthings for them.

In certain respects Christmas toys mirror aspects of American life and culture. For example, a large proportion of those sold during the holidays are mechanical and are often miniature replicas of machines used by adults, as in the case of engines, fire trucks, airplanes, and bulldozers. These playthings are graded by age and adjusted to the conventional adult roles of the two sexes. Thus doctors' kits are provided for boys and visiting nurses' kits for the girls. Toys are also used as a medium for training the young in motor skills and knowledge of language. This is evident in the sale of peg boards, alphabet blocks, and the like. The very young are provided with playthings which encourage fantasy life through such items as marionettes, Teddy bears, and other animals, but these toys are noticeably lacking for those above the age of seven or eight. Soldiers, guns, rockets, and space suits reflect perhaps both the troubled world situation and the imaginative fringe of scientific invention and discovery. The "cowboy cult" continues to find popular expression in a variety of toys which duplicate the dress and equipment of those "at home on the range."

In the main, American toys and playthings give but slight encouragement to the development of imagination and fantasy in the young. This accords with the prevailing attitudes of a pragmatic people and culture. On the other hand, our toys exhibit great emphasis on the development of utilitarian skills which may have value in later years. Children are also encouraged through toys to familiarize themselves with standardized social roles such as those of the cowboy, the soldier, the circus performer, the truck driver, and so on. This gives a definite "educational" bias to the American child's toys, and probably explains, in some measure, the adult enthusiasm for buying Christmas presents for children.

Commercial exploitation of Christmas customs has been successful also in the case of the Christmas card. This convention grew in popularity after Prang introduced his famous cards in Boston in the 1870's, and is observed by many millions each Christmas. The National Association of Greeting Card Publishers believes that over 1,500,000,000 Christmas cards are sent each year.[14] A conservative estimate of the retail value of this number of cards would approximate $100,-000,000. Designs on Christmas cards usually employ the symbols of the Nativity, Santa Claus's visit, children, animals, and familiar decorative items or scenes. These include holly, ivy, mistletoe, trees, wintry scenes in the country, family dinners, and carolers. Some cards express no definite relation either to the religious or to the folk character of the occasion. Most messages on Christmas cards repeat stereotyped greetings, with some being ornately worded and others restricted to "Merry Christmas and a Happy New Year." Commercial success in exploiting this Christmas custom has been based on the provision of a wide variety of cards that meet the tastes and financial resources of different social groups.

The Christmas tree also has an important place in the holiday business. Many millions of families and numerous business, charitable, and fraternal organizations buy, set up, and decorate about 28,000,000 trees each year.[15] Of this number, about 5,000,000 are imported, chiefly from Canada. The majority of our trees come from privately owned lands, though about 13 per cent are cut on the public domain. Some twenty-five different varieties of trees are grown for the Christmas trade. However, the balsam fir and Douglas fir together account for about 57 per cent of all Christmas trees used in this country. The economic importance of the Christmas tree is considerable. Sowder estimates that "the trees produced in a recent year would make a 20 to 50 million dollar industry, according to whether values are based on the wholesale or retail prices quoted." [16] If the value of decorations, stands, and so on, is added to the cost of the trees, it is apparent that the national Christmas-tree custom supports an important seasonal industry.

Effects on Employment and Industrial Disputes

Commercial exploitation of Christmas affects retail employment during December, and manufacture of merchandise for the holiday business involves the labor of large numbers of workers throughout other months of the year. The annual increase in December employment in trade is followed by a sharp decline in January and February.[17] Occupations such as manufacturing, mining, transportation, communications, and agriculture either drop or increase only slightly in the number of workers employed during December.

Another indication of the influence of Christmas appears in the small number of labor disputes begun in December. Both strikes and lockouts fall off during this month and rise sharply in the next two months. The December figures vary so sharply from those of November and January as to suggest that special influences of the "Christmas spirit" account for the low number of disputes begun in this month. Table IV shows monthly variations in these for six-month periods.

Not only do few disputes begin in December, but in addition the number of workers involved is low in those initiated during this month. Furthermore, figures on strikes occurring in the United States during the years 1901–1905 and 1915–

TABLE IV. MONTHLY FIGURES ON INDUSTRIAL DISPUTES BEGUN FOR THE
YEARS 1946–52 (STRIKES AND LOCKOUTS) [18]

YEAR	SEPT.	OCT.	NOV.	DEC.	JAN.	FEB.
1946–47	499	516	344	163	321	296
1947–48	219	219	178	119	221	266
1948–49	299	256	216	144	274	240
1949–50	290	250	200	170	248	210
1950–51	521	550	329	218	442	345
1951–52	457	487	305	186	438	403

1937 show that the index for these was usually lowest during the month of December.[19]

The significance of Christmas to laboring groups is also indicated by the fact that December 25th is invariably stipulated as a holiday in contracts between management and unions.[20] In some occupations, such as women's clothing, bakery, wholesale and retail trade, trucking, technical and professional work, employees usually receive the major holidays with pay. However, in mining, manufacturing, and construction work, these holidays are given, but without compensation. Various provisions are inserted in union agreements concerning extra pay when employees are required to do maintenance and emergency work at Christmas.

The Christmas Bonus

The varied role of the Christmas festival in the national economy is demonstrated further by recent developments related to the "Christmas bonus." This practice differs from the usual commercial exploitation of the occasion, but the distinction is probably one of degree rather than of kind.

For a number of years, many employers have used Christmas as an occasion appropriate for giving their employees an annual bonus. According to a report made in 1951 by the National Industrial Conference Board, in 1950 Christmas bonus plans were in operation in chemicals, electrical equipment, machinery, paper, textiles, banks, and trust companies.[21] Both large and small firms gave holiday bonuses. Plans varied considerably in that some gave substantially all employees a fixed sum, while others gave a percentage of earnings. Eligibility was specified in all plans, which even included pensioners. The amounts ranged from five to several hundred dollars. Some firms gave merchandise, but money appears to be the most popular Christmas gift. Most firms have based their decision to give a Christmas bonus on their business success each year. This criterion has also determined the amount to be given.

Management had assumed that granting a bonus was discretionary on its part, but this assumption was rudely challenged in 1950 in the Niles-Bement-Pond case.[22] The firm announced that it was instituting a new retirement plan which would cost considerable money. For that reason it felt unable to give its employees the usual Christmas or year-end bonus. However, the company planned to give each employee a Christmas money gift computed on the basis of one dollar for each year of service with the firm. Under the proposed plan no employee would receive less than five dollars. The union representing the employees requested the company to negotiate the 1950 bonus.[23] Niles-Bement-Pond refused to do so, and the union appealed the case to the National Labor Relations Board.

The board issued an intermediate decision in August of 1951, confirmed by a final one in December of the same year, which supported the position of the union. It ordered Niles-Bement-Pond Company to bargain with respect to the Christmas bonus and forbade it taking any action on the bonus without consulting the union's representatives. The majority decision of the board held that the bonus was a Christmas one in name only. They regarded it chiefly as a "year-end" bonus which through repetition had become a regular part of the employees' wage expectancy and, therefore, subject to the usual collective bargaining procedures. One member of the board dissented, asserting that the bonus was a true "Christmas gift," and said:

To bestow *freely* is the *sine qua non* of a gift. Particularly at the Christmas season men are moved to make gifts to those they cherish, to those they employ, and to those less fortunate . . . if we say that an employer must obtain permission to make a Christmas gift to his employees and must be willing to haggle about whether he should make any gift or about the value of his gift, we have in large measure destroyed the concept, spirit and practice of Christmas giving in the labor-management field . . . a genuine Christmas gift has no place at the bargaining table.[24]

What appears to have happened is that the term "Christmas bonus" has been misapplied to the practice of sharing profits with employees during "good times." As a result many workers have come to expect a bonus each year, and no longer interpret it as a sign of managerial good will and generosity. On the other hand, employers have considered this instance of profit sharing to be a privilege of management and an evidence of personal interest in their employees. Confusion in the matter was to be expected because relations of Christmas donors and recipients are different from those of worker and employer. The former are personal and informal, but the latter are formal and contractual. The Christmas bonus exhibits attributes of both these sets of relations, and divergent interpretation of its character was unavoidable.

It is worth noting, in passing, that the idea of a Christmas bonus for employees has not evoked a reciprocal inclination on their part to "give" additional time or productivity to their employers at Christmas. This suggests that employees define their relations to management as contractual at Christmas as well as at other times.

"Commercializing Christmas"—An Evaluation

Many Americans believe that the commercial aspects of Christmas are destroying much of its traditional significance. In addition, devout Christians fear that the festival is interpreted to the public chiefly as an occasion for buying and selling, giving and receiving, rather than for celebrating the birth of Christ. Others object to the merchant's Christmas, not on religious grounds but because they believe it has transformed a folk festival into a period of maniacal shopping. However, some find the commercial note to their liking and consider it as natural as the religious and festive ones. Such varied attitudes toward gainful use of the occasion warrant further discussion.

The commercialization of Christmas—and of other national festivals—is rooted in the business character of our economy. Thus the struggle for profits is predicated on a regular demand for goods, and the holiday season can provide this each year. Further, the intrinsic spirit of business enterprise seeks ever increasing profits. This leads merchants to unceasing efforts to surpass the sales of previous years. For example, an advertising executive spoke before the National Retail Dry Goods Association in the fall of 1951 and dwelt on the prospects of Christmas business. He asserted, "Stores will have to raise their advertising percentages if they expect to match and *beat* last year's figures." [25]

Not only do business firms regard the acquisition of profits as their principal goal; they also seek them in a rational, and not in a haphazard, manner. Exploitation of holidays and festivals is but one instance of the application of rationality to the merchandizing process. This is achieved by deliberately manipulating the traditional social values and emotions of the occasion so as to encourage public buying. Because the festival evokes powerful family sentiments, stimulates greater affection for children and a strong sense of brotherhood, the public is peculiarly susceptible to some kinds of Christmas advertising. Newspapers, radio broadcasts, telecasts, decorations, music, and the professional Santa Claus conspire to persuade all that the occasion requires gifts. Department stores offer advice on the types of presents appropriate to various relationships and even provide specialized personnel to assist shoppers in selecting them.

However, retail merchants vary greatly in exploiting the festival. Some use the Christian imagery of the Nativity in ways which debase its spiritual significance and outrage good taste, but this is, on the whole, rare. In most instances advertising is restricted to using the folk symbols of Santa Claus, carolers, or family gatherings to promote the sale of items bearing a specific trade name. Moreover, some firms use these symbols only as decorative background to personify the season, and do not attempt to promote sales by reference to traditional imagery. Not all retail establishments are equally inclined to commercialize Christmas through this medium.

Nevertheless, because most stores do use the festival for gain, in at least a limited fashion, the individual merchant seldom dares ignore or slight its commercial possibilities. The exigencies of competition force him to recognize the financial rewards of exploiting the festival and provide a strong argument for perpetuating the practice. Thus the general acceptance of holiday exploitation has forced many businessmen to engage in merchandising customs repugnant to their personal values and tastes. Some have rebelled and actively supported community efforts to "keep Christ in Christmas." However, such sporadic opposition to commercializing the occasion has not been noticeably effective.

Though the manipulation of the festival for gain has been successful and is tolerated by the public, it has also provoked considerable resentment. This exasperation finds expression in grumbling about prices, traffic conditions, the competitiveness of buyers, and the lack of time for buying and mailing gifts. One hears frequent declaration that the celebration has changed for the worse. Concrete evidence of dissatisfaction appears in "letters to the Editor" columns of newspapers during the Christmas season. These condemn public failure to understand the religious nature of the occasion, the ubiquity of gift exchanging, the bad taste of holiday advertising, and the covetousness both of children and of adults at Christmas. Contributors to these columns often insist that the festival has lost its sacred, brotherly character and has become an annual commercial orgy.

In the same vein newspaper editorials lament: "So the holiday season is with us again. We face once again the unrestrained joy of Christmas shopping." Cartoons announce the approach of the festive season in a manner calculated to warn, rather than to delight, the public.

Most of the hostility aroused by commercial influences in the festival is directed at retail merchants, which is ironic, because manufacturers and wholesale dealers are equally involved in making money through Christmas trade, but receive little criticism. They are protected by the fact that they have little direct contact with the public during the "shopping season," and have little to do with the annual blast of holiday promotion. For these reasons they avoid the onus of responsibility for commercializing the festival.

Those who criticize the business manipulation of Christmas insist that such activities profane its religious character, increase covetousness, slight the importance of the family in the celebration, and ignore its implications for human brotherhood. Some of these objections have substance, while others appear very labored.

So far as the devout Christian is concerned, commercial influences in the festival do tend to nullify its religious character. For instance, the implications of the Nativity are spiritual and selfless, while most of those of the "Christmas shopping season" are materialistic and acquisitive. As a consequence, the annual juxtaposition of these divergent values produces emotional conflict in those who attempt to follow simultaneously these different sets of precepts. For example, preoccupation with gift exchanging is likely to interfere with veneration of the Nativity.

However, it is difficult to believe that commercial manipulation promotes neglect of the familial and fraternal aspects of the occasion. On the contrary, there is considerable evidence of a marked increase in charity and generosity each Christmas. Furthermore, family unity appears more in evidence during this festival than at any other time of the year. If these values are cherished in daily life, they will not be neglected at Christmas.

Some allege that commercial exploitation increases covetousness during the holidays. They usually accuse others of such greed, but seldom admit to the same fault in themselves, which suggests that the complaint masks some other dissatisfaction. Perhaps those who dislike the Big Swap or dread its financial consequences, yet are unwilling to abandon the custom, displace their anger onto commercial influences.

In addition, a good deal of hostility springing from quite unrelated sources is aimed at acquisitive influences in the holiday. For instance, many persons expect each Christmas to be a satisfying emotional experience but encounter frequent disappointment on this score. Parents recall happy festivals of their childhood but shrink from confronting the duties and minor irritations of "having Christmas" for their children. They can no longer anticipate a relaxed, permissive holiday, but must plan, buy, and mail gifts and cards. Under these circumstances elders experience a sense of deprivation and annoyance which is blamed on business exploitation rather than on a change in their role in the festival.

In spite of frequent condemnation, business manipulation of Christmas continues and shows some tendencies to broaden its area of influence. In one generation the American public has grown accustomed to pre-holiday advertising, the professional Santa Claus, store decorations inside and out, "canned" music on the streets, the office party, and especially to preoccupation with Christmas shopping. These things are so thoroughly accepted as trappings of the season that their absence would divest the festival of much of its attractiveness. As a matter of fact, many adults accept the commercial "props" of the holiday with tolerance and even with enthusiasm. This group probably outnumbers those who dislike commercializing the occasion.

It should be added that children appear to be delighted with the mercantile backdrop of Christmas. Their credulity is able to encompass even the sight of different Santas in department stores without losing faith in "his" existence. Those born after 1920 have become accustomed to business influences in the public celebration, and it is doubtful if they will view commercialization of the occasion with a jaundiced eye.

Thus, there seems little reason to doubt that commercial exploitation has popularized the folk aspects of Christmas, even though it has done so at the expense of its spiritual significance. Unfortunately, it has also promoted a widespread inclination to appraise Christmas in materialistic, acquisitive terms. To counteract this common attitude, it has become standard practice for the Christian churches of the United States to reiterate annually that Christmas is celebrated primarily in observance of the birth of Christ and to insist that secular festivities are secondary to its spiritual implications. This fact suggests that the folk and temporal qualities of the celebration have gained ascendancy over its religious ones, and it is likely that commercial influences have played an important role in bringing this about.

However, if humanitarian and charitable acts at Christmas are construed as a concrete manifestation of the spirit of Christ, then business influences are less open to the charge of secularizing the occasion. This is said in the belief that Christmas generosity is characteristic of business firms in nearly all American communities, even though the motivation for such beneficence may not be rooted in Christian teachings. Since such charity expresses values which are congruent with those of Christianity, it indicates a degree of accord in the participation of church and business in the annual festival. For this reason, though the Christmas activity of business groups generally tends to secularize the celebration, indirectly it also supports its traditional religious values.

CHAPTER V

Social Aspects of Christmas Art

Festivals are preserved through art forms, and Christmas has accumulated a rich and distinctive body of songs, stories, poems, pictures, and plays. These embody its traditions and meanings and transmit them from generation to generation. In this country they also mirror important episodes in the development of the festival and reveal the steady growth of secular influences in the national Christmas.

The major portion of traditional Christmas art has long been concerned with the Nativity theme, and this fact probably retarded its development somewhat in the United States. Because of Puritan opposition, the flow of English and Continental Christmas art to the American colonies was checked at a time when cultural foundations were being laid. As a result, such historical resources were wanting in this country. In fact, the United States did not begin to develop native art in keeping with the festival until the nineteenth century.

Consequently, American Christmas art of this period is neither so abundant nor so varied as that of England and several European countries. Nevertheless, some of its contributions have merit, especially those in literature, and have spread to other countries. They also provide background for understanding the later development of "popular" Christmas art.

Traditional Christmas Art

As the evangelical Protestant denominations gradually accepted the observance of Christmas during the 1800's, they sought to develop appropriate religious services for both the church and the church schools. This encouraged the composition of music and songs and the production of cantatas and pageants for Christmas programs. Under this stimulation a number of well known hymns were written in the United States during the nineteenth century. These included such songs as "O Little Town of Bethlehem," by Phillips Brooks (1868); "It Came Upon a Midnight Clear," by Edmund H. Sears (1850); and "We Three Kings of Orient Are," by John W. Hopkins, Jr. (1859). In addition, Christmas plays, cantatas, and pageants began to appear about 1890. Among these were: *The Real Santa Claus*, by J. L. Hall and C. A. Miles; *The Shepherd King*, by J. L. Hall and E. D. Yale; *Why the Chimes Rang*, dramatized by Elizabeth McFadden; *The Next-Door House*, by Margaret Cropper, and others. Church schools often employed both Nativity and Santa Claus elements in Christmas programs. However, this provoked considerable criticism as the desire grew to eliminate the folk elements from the religious observance.

On the other hand, the Episcopalian, Lutheran, Dutch Reformed, and Roman Catholic churches and the German sects retained their traditional forms, music, and songs in observing Christmas, while their members also preserved familiarity with folk customs. These historical cultural resources have done much to maintain the vitality of the celebration among groups such as the Pennsylvania Germans. Their manger scenes, gardens, and Christmas Eve musical services are a happy blending of tradition, folk art, and seasonal joy which endows the festival with unusual charm.

During the nineteenth century Christmas was a subject which also drew the attention of American writers and painters. Washington Irving wrote romanticized accounts of Christmas celebrations in the English countryside, and Clement Clarke Moore created a new folk tale in his "A Visit from St. Nicholas." James Russell Lowell, Longfellow, Eugene Field, and many others wrote Christmas poetry, while Bret Harte, James K. Spaulding, Kate Douglas Wiggin, F. Hopkinson Smith, and Louisa May Alcott—to mention only a few—wrote stories of the festival which have become favorites.[1] Some took the Nativity as their focus of interest, others extolled the virtues of humanitarianism at Christmas, while still others elaborated variations of the Santa Claus theme. Their stories and poems had a pronounced folk quality even though created by a single individual.

In addition, a number of American painters and engravers experimented with pictures of Santa Claus during the nineteenth century. Prominent among them were Weir, Nast, Smith, Darley, and Schell. Their portrayals of the gift bringer frequently bordered on caricature. Nast was most successful in creating a pictorial conception of Santa Claus which personified his folk qualities and captured public favor. Since his time there have been no important additions to the folk figures of Christmas pictorial art, with the possible exception of Rudolph the Red-Nosed Reindeer.

During the last century illustrations of the Nativity used in this country were mostly reproductions of famous European paintings by artists such as Dürer, Gentile da Fabriano, Bosch, Memling, Veronese, and Patinir. The prestige of the old masters and the almost hallowed character of their Nativity paintings discouraged American artists from undertaking new interpretations of this theme. In addition, Protestant opposition to the observance of Christmas disappeared quite slowly in some parts of the United States.

The twentieth century has produced well known Christmas stories by such American writers as Henry van Dyke, Rupert Hughes, Zona Gale, Julia Peterkin, O. Henry, Ring Lardner,

Roark Bradford, and others.[2] Most of their tales are concerned
with implications of the Nativity. The twentieth century
has also seen the appearance of poems on both religious and
folk aspects of Christmas. W. H. Auden's *For the Time Being*
is by all odds the most discerning treatment of Christmas to
appear in verse form during the present century. It explores
the spiritual meaning of the Nativity in lines filled with elusive
beauty and disturbing images. In a telling passage, Auden describes modern man's incapacity for grasping the import of
the Nativity:

                                                    Once again
As in previous years we have seen the actual Vision and failed
To do more than entertain it as an agreeable
Possibility, once again we have sent Him away
Begging though to remain His disobedient servant,
The promising child who cannot keep His word for long.[3]

E. E. Cummings's *Santa Claus—A Morality* is provocative,
but only tangential to Christmas. An allegory in verse, it
deals with the traditional figure of the gift bringer but in a
new vein. Cummings lifts Santa Claus quite out of his role as
the patron of children and uses him to engage in a philosophical battle with the ideology of modern science. This is a
clear departure from the traditional use of this symbol.

The contemporary significance and popularity of Christmas have stimulated modern painters to attempt to portray
the subject in a serious manner. Most of their efforts concern
some aspect of the Nativity account, and there is a tendency
to cling to the traditional mode of representation. However,
Edmund Lewandowski's "Three Kings" offers a new interpretation of this theme. Other American artists who have
portrayed Christmas motifs with great competence are Fred
Conway, Louis Bosa, Laurence Sisson, and Robert Gates.[4]
These painters offer unstereotyped interpretations of the
festival and deal with its modern as well as with its folklore

aspects. They are not limited to the inevitable star, shepherds, or animals associated with the occasion. It is significant that they find the tale of Santa Claus lacking in artistic interest but continue to be challenged by the Nativity account.

Serious music by American composers of the twentieth century has been devoted to the Nativity story and shows no indication of exploiting other themes in the Christmas festival. The most recent and meritorious example of this type of Christmas music is Gian-Carlo Menotti's *Amahl and the Night Visitors*, a short opera performed for the first time on Christmas Eve in 1951.[5] This work narrates an episode in the journey of the Three Kings who seek the Christ Child. Most of the music is programmatic and simply recounts the development of its plot. It is conventional, original, and rewarding. Like most Nativity music, it creates a sense of anticipation directed toward the central event of the occasion.

When all is said and done, the traditional varieties of Christmas art are concerned with the biblical and folklore character of the festival, and not with its contemporary aspect. They symbolize its relatively unchanging elements and permanent values and preserve its conventional forms. Because of this, the accepted examples of holiday art will seldom mirror fugitive shifts in public taste or the changing role of Christmas in American life. However, in very recent decades a new type of art has begun to develop which seizes on diffuse, but neglected, aspects of Christmas and exploits them for commercial ends.

"Popular" Art

There is a new type of Christmas art which may be termed "popular" in contrast to serious or fine art because it seeks primarily commercial success and, to achieve this end, deliberately uses themes and symbols that are simple and liked

by many.[6] It is of special value in studying Christmas because
it reveals the interrelations between the festival and contemporary life. Popular Christmas art is, of course, but one example of this type of artistic activity.

Behind it appear the conditioning factors of a business
economy, urbanism, a high degree of literacy, and scientific
advances in communication. These have brought in an era of
mass communication and entertainment which has already
had considerable influence on modern American life. Concretely, this has come about through the provision of inexpensive books for children, the radio song, story, or drama,
the television program, the motion picture, and the comic
strip. These media condition the appearance and, in part,
the character of popular art. They also serve the interests of
advertising by providing familiar symbols to increase public
demand for goods. Popular art usually employs conventional
figures, ideas, and values, and seldom creates new ones. It
uses stereotypes to simplify ideas, characters, and situations.
It is a type of art that often exhibits considerable technical
competence; but its primary purpose is to make money rather
than to create beauty, to edify or to educate the public.
Popular Christmas art must be understood in light of this fact.

During the past twenty-five years, Christmas has been exploited extensively in popular songs, stories, plays, and pictures. Radio, motion pictures, and comic books are the media
which bring these versions of holiday themes to the public
and demonstrate the existence of a powerful new influence in
the celebration. For the most part the folk and secular lore
of the festival has dominated the creations of popular art
because of their commercial effectiveness, though occasionally a theme with religious implications is presented. This
dissemination of Christmas themes by mass media of entertainment for profitable ends has had a considerable, though inde-
terminate, influence on the festival and on its place in American life.

For one thing, it has greatly increased the public's superficial knowledge of Christmas lore, while at the same time selectively restricting attention to those aspects of the celebration having a wide appeal. Thus Christmas narratives exemplifying the themes of kindness, brotherhood, and humility, or insisting on the ultimate rewards of piety and generosity, find ready acceptance because they express traditional values of American culture. On the other hand, Christmas themes not welcomed by Americans receive only slight acknowledgment, or may be completely ignored.[7] This is characteristically true of the traditional threat to children that Santa Claus will not bring presents if they misbehave. The threat is purely formal and is often omitted because it is at variance with American permissiveness to children at Christmas. The incessant repetition of these standardized holiday motifs in song, story, and picture cannot fail to affect the character and meaning of the festival, especially since much of it is directed at children.

The close association of popular Christmas art with advertising and merchandising might be expected to encourage novelty, variety, and innovation, since public taste and likes change frequently. This is precisely what happens. Nearly every year a new song, figure, or story appears which is relevant to the traditional Christmas but contrived for a mass market.

Some of these gain public favor and survive for a period of years. This suggests that they possess latent psychological appeal as well as entertainment virtues. One of the best known and most interesting examples of popular Christmas art concerns a young deer with a shiny red nose.

"Rudolph the Red-Nosed Reindeer"

The tale of Rudolph the Red-Nosed Reindeer is a very important addition to the folk celebration of Christmas. It has become popular in a short time, and there are signs that this "rejected" deer will be fused with Santa Claus in Christmas lore. In some respects the story of Rudolph is an elaboration of elements contained in Moore's "A Visit from St. Nicholas," while in others it brings new traits and meaning to the traditional account.

The story, cast in a loose poetic style, was written in 1939 by Robert L. May, who was employed in the advertising department of Montgomery Ward & Company, a well known mail-order house. He was assigned the task of developing a Christmas "animal story" which could be distributed by the branches of his firm as a "give-away" during the Christmas season of 1939. It was so popular that over 2,400,000 copies of the first give-away edition were distributed that year.[8] For various reasons, the firm did not use the story again for several years. However, it reappeared in 1946, when about 3,500,000 copies were distributed. In 1947 the story was brought out on a commercial basis and has since continued to have a very large sale.

In 1949 a song entitled "Rudolph the Red-Nosed Reindeer" was composed by Johnny Marks and quickly became popular. It was recorded by several well known singers and was the leading musical sales item of the year. The recordings made by such public favorites as Gene Autry and Bing Crosby undoubtedly had much to do with promoting public interest and liking both for the song and for the tale.

The story and its creation throw light on popular art and on contemporary American culture. Rudolph was a young reindeer marked by the possession of a large, shiny red nose which caused him to be the butt of jokes played on him by reindeer companions. He was kept out of their games and suffered as a "rejected" reindeer. One Christmas Eve the sky was unusually overcast, and Santa Claus had great difficulty in delivering his presents because he could not see clearly. He stumbled several times until he arrived by chance at Rudolph's room, where he was surprised to notice a glow of light. This

came from the bright red nose of Rudolph, who was fast
asleep, hoping for a Christmas present. Santa Claus decided
to ask Rudolph to lead his reindeer team, awakened the young
deer, and asked him to guide his magical sleigh. Rudolph was
flattered, agreed to go with Santa Claus, and thoughtfully
left a note for his parents telling them the reason for his
absence, and was off at the head of Santa's team.

Rudolph's nose provided sufficient light to read street signs
and house numbers so that Santa Claus was able to complete
his deliveries just before dawn broke. Then Rudolph guided
the team back to the North and whirled in from the sky before the eyes of those companions who had laughed at his
red nose and made cruel sport of him in the past. Santa Claus
was loud in his praises of Rudolph, called him the best reindeer ever to guide his famous sleigh, and asked him to lead
it the next year. Rudolph was overcome with joy, and the
reindeer who had previously made fun of him now sought his
company and favor. Thus virtue was rewarded and a physical handicap converted into a valuable attribute. The tale
ended with the conventional Moore line, "A Merry Christmas
to All and to All a Good Night."

The sudden and continuing popularity of this story calls
for explanation. May, the author, was an experienced advertising man who undertook to write a Christmas story for
children as a regular part of his work. He decided to organ-
ize the narrative around the "ugly duckling" motif. May believes that he was influenced by his own childhood in the
selection of this theme.[9]

After careful consideration of possible animals, he decided
to use the reindeer, partly because the creature was already
connected with the traditional Moore story of Santa Claus.
The name of Rudolph was selected by a "desire for allitera-
tion, a process of rejecting other "*R* names," [10] and by in-
spired guessing. Then the author made up his mind to relate
the story's happy ending to Santa Claus. This blossomed into

a decision to give the reindeer some trait which would cause him to be shunned, yet would be of great value to Santa Claus. It was necessary to do so in order to conform to the "ugly duckling" theme. Though strength or speed might have been useful to Santa Claus, they would not lay Rudolph open to the ridicule essential to his role. It then occurred to the author that Santa Claus traveled at night, when the light was poor, and this suggested the idea that Rudolph might be given large, shiny eyes which could see in the dark. However, this was rejected as not being a sufficient cause for ridicule.

Finally, he fixed on the large nose, which has long been considered a legitimate subject of ridicule in Western culture and has been exploited by such well known figures as W. C. Fields and Jimmy Durante. He decided to make the nose large and shiny to provide light for Santa Claus, and red to inspire ridicule. The plot and characters developed in this manner were related to the annual visit of Santa Claus. The story was written in prose, then converted into verse. Its appeal to children and to many adults was immediate and marked.

By way of explanation, it should be noted that the reindeer has long been a favorite animal figure in the United States. In addition to its magical associations already established by Moore's poem, it is a creature with which children can identify themselves. Many youngsters, like Rudolph, have some distinguishing weakness which might subject them to ridicule from their playmates. The transformation of Rudolph's stigma into a rare talent appealed to children who had vicariously shared Rudolph's sorrows and were pleased that he was able to assist Santa Claus, their gift bringer.

In May's story Santa Claus was different from the St. Nicholas of Moore's poem in that he was not omnipotent, could not see perfectly in the darkness, and sought the help of a young reindeer (read "child"). Symbolically, the small child came to the aid of the powerful parents and exhibited unexpected powers. The focus of Moore's poem is upon Santa Claus, while May's poem centers on the figure of Rudolph, who is, in a sense, a child figure able to aid the parents. To some degree, the possibility that children identify with Rudolph offers an explanation of the sudden and continuing popularity of the story, the song, and the various pictorial representations of this now-famous deer. Of course, it is also true that the melody of the song and illustrations of the story promoted its popularity.

Apparently memories of rejection in childhood led the author unconsciously to select a folklore motif which reflected these experiences. In addition, at the time of writing the story about Rudolph, he was laboring under a heavy burden of domestic and personal problems. These provided him with a reality basis for unconsciously identifying with a legendary figure (the ugly duckling) which also suffered great hardship but eventually found happiness through his tribulations.

Children's fondness for Rudolph is attested by the following account which appeared in the *Milwaukee Journal* for December 26, 1950. The story also suggests that Rudolph has acquired that quality of real existence which characterizes the more lasting figures of folklore:

It seems that a successful deer hunter, with his quarry on the fender, stopped en route home to regale his cronies with the story of his triumph. The telling took longer than he planned, and certain low comedy characters utilized the pause to sow the seeds of his undoing. They sent for red paint and while the hunter recounted the glories of his hunt inside, they painted the nose of his slain buck a ruby red.

At this point, by no accident, the youngsters were homeward bound from school. And the enemies of our hero, not satisfied with leaving the red-nosed buck out there in naked view, stopped some of the moppets and horrified them with a whispered alarm. "Look! Rudolph."

By the time our hero emerged, fifty youngsters were dug in for battle equipped with snowballs, rocks and righteous wrath. Well, he escaped with his life, and on Christmas Eve, it turned out that Rudolph was all right after all. So now the tale can be told.

Rudolph seems to express an important theme of American culture through his success in becoming the *lead* reindeer of Santa's team, which may not be unrelated to the American faith in every person's ability to succeed if he can only "get a break." Light is also thrown on his cultural character if he is regarded as a "guiding animal." [11] This folklore type has appeared widely in both primitive and classical folk tales concerning animals that have helped men to find food, safety, gold, and hiding places. These tales repeat in diverse forms the theme of animals guiding man to good fortune or to safety when in danger. Rudolph clearly plays this role in relation to Santa Claus.

Rudolph has become a favorite with the young to such an extent that in the New York *Daily News* for December 23, 1950, a correspondent wrote, "Pretty soon children will think it [Christmas] is a red-nosed reindeer's birthday." Furthermore, his general acceptance as an established holiday figure is suggested by the fact that he appears in public places, department stores, and parades almost as frequently as Santa Claus. Children send numerous letters to him each year through newspaper columns and demand a variety of articles, toys, and clothing that bear the Rudolph label. The story and song have achieved considerable popularity in several European countries, Australia, and Canada, and have been accepted to a degree even in South American countries which celebrate a different type of Christmas. Apparently the Rudolph story embodies qualities that have a somewhat universal appeal.

In spite of the fact that commercial motives prompted the

deliberate creation of the Rudolph story, it has achieved popularity beyond that warranted by its narrative qualities. However, it remains to be seen if the Rudolph tale will survive the annual orgy of exploitation in pre-Christmas advertising. If the story of the red-nosed reindeer provides important emotional satisfactions to young children, this will promote its incorporation into the folk Christmas, and Rudolph may enjoy a long life in spite of extensive commercial manipulation. In addition, the author of the Rudolph story has made a conscious effort to associate his reindeer with Santa Claus, both in the original story and in the 1951 sequel, "Rudolph's Second Christmas." This may result in a linking of the two figures in the public mind. If that occurs Santa Claus will tend to "carry" the figure of Rudolph and will also receive reinforcement from it.

Christmas offers abundant resources for the development of popular art, especially if the varied national celebrations of Europe are put to use. These celebrations provide a rich body of figures, themes, and episodes, some of which could be adapted to the predilections of American culture. In addition, popular art has already begun to work changes in the imagery of the folk Christmas by introducing newcomers such as Rudolph to the gallery of traditional figures. It has also produced other Christmas symbols, stories, and songs, some of which will be discussed shortly, but the red-nosed reindeer appears most likely to become a lasting addition to the folk festival.

Miracle on 34th Street

It was almost inevitable that, sooner or later, an American writer would treat the theme of Santa Claus's existence with apparent seriousness. Valentine Davies has done this in an amusing and insightful story called *Miracle on 34th Street*

(1947). This tale not only demonstrates, with mock gravity, the existence of Santa Claus but also proves that there is no conflict between the spirit of Christmas and business enterprise. A dash of romance and some fun at the expense of applied psychology and "career" women provide it with appeals tailored to public liking. This is in keeping with its character as popular art.

Miracle on 34th Street is an ingenious effort at literary exploitation of popular Christmas themes and symbols. It combats skepticism about Santa Claus and portrays a modern revival of belief in him where this might least be expected—in a large department store in New York City. Faith in Santa Claus, once renewed, softens commercial rivalry between the heads of two competing stores and causes a spirit of helpfulness to supplant greed and competition during the Christmas season.

The initial commercial success and frequent revivals of the story in film and radio versions indicate its popularity,[12] which can be attributed to the perennial attraction of tales about Santa Claus as well as to the skillful craftsmanship apparent both in the novel and in the motion picture. The film has been well received both in England and in France, and the novel has been translated into French very recently. A short synopsis of the story will indicate its treatment of Christmas motifs.

An elderly man, named Kris Kringle, has been told by the house physician of an old people's home that he must leave the institution since he continues to assert that he is Santa Claus. He is advised by the kindly doctor to enter a "mental" institution, even though he is entirely harmless, because he lacks any means of financial support. Kris rejects the suggestion, leaves the home, and goes to New York City, arriving there on the day of the Thanksgiving parade sponsored by Macy's Department Store. Kris is persuaded to play the role of Santa Claus in the parade when the original one is discovered drunk. He fits the role so well that he is employed as a professional Santa Claus for the Christmas season at Macy's.

Though he is very successful in his new position, he brings consternation to the store officials by advising customers to purchase goods not available at Macy's at competing stores. To everyone's surprise, Kris's unorthodox advice is imitated by other stores, which are moved by the "Christmas spirit" to send customers to Macy's, so that commercial advantage results from Kringle's naïve act. Kris meets the divorcée Doris Walker, a career woman in the publicity department of Macy's, and her daughter Susan, a precocious child who has been taught to suppress her fantasy life. He also meets imaginative and impractical Fred Gayley, who is in love with Doris. On the other hand, Doris prides herself on being realistic, and has reared Susan from this point of view. Kris becomes friendly with these three people, begins to win Susan's devotion, and attempts to awaken in her a liking for imaginary persons such as fairies and Santa Claus. Though Doris is displeased at Kris's influence on Susan, she is uneasy in the face of his calm assurance that he *is* Santa Claus. Nevertheless, she is pleased at her daughter's improved ability to play with other children and at her increased air of contentment.

However, Kris antagonizes the store psychologist, becomes involved in a serious quarrel with him over belief in the existence of Santa Claus, and is sent to Bellevue Hospital for psychiatric observation. Fred, his lawyer, who arranges for a sanity hearing in a municipal court, has to find some authoritative person or agency which accepts Kris's identity to prevent him from being committed permanently. Kris is saved because Susan has written to him, addressing the letter to Santa Claus, in care of the court at which the hearing is being held. A mail clerk, surrounded by thousands of letters addressed to Santa Claus, decides to send them to Kris at the court address. This is done in time for the judge to declare that Santa Claus exists and, because Kris is identified by the United States Postal Service as Santa Claus, to declare him sane. Kris leaves the courtroom at once, since it is Christmas Eve, and disappears until the next day. On Christmas morning the reindeer at the municipal zoo are discovered lathered and tired. Doris and Fred acknowledge their love for each other and plan to marry, which will enable Susan to lead the life of a normal child. Kris returns to the old people's home, now that he has been adjudged sane. He has accomplished his mission of reviving the world's faith in the existence of Santa Claus in spite of commercialism, hardness of heart, and doubt.

The tale involves a strong profession of belief in the good will associated with Christmas, as well as of faith in the existence of Santa Claus, who personifies the season. It gives the story an affirmative quality associated with the traditional Christmas. *Miracle on 34th Street* recommends the time-honored recipe of the "spirit of Christmas" even for commercial rivals, and, since this formula turns out to be financially profitable, it provides convincing proof of the value of faith and imagination. The omnipotence of Santa Claus is suggested by the fact that Kris rises above the probings of psychiatry when he deliberately gives wrong answers to questions asked him on admission to the hospital. However, the proof of "Santa Claus's" existence and Kris's identity were established by a judicial ruling which involved legal trickery and by familial pressure on both the judge and the prosecutor. A mixture of respect and amusement at courtroom procedures is apparent in the scenes in which the law is tortured into agreement with popular sentiments.

One finds again in this story the theme of Santa Claus's disillusionment with human beings and the restoration of belief in his importance through the faith of children. This is in keeping with the earlier treatment of the same theme by

Ednah Proctor Clarke in "The Revolt of Santa Claus" (1901)
and with the radio burlesque of the motif by Fred Allen in
his skit "Santa Won't Ride Tonight" broadcast in December,
1947. Davies's treatment of Santa Claus is another instance of
portraying the figure as still possessed of magical powers
though he is becoming increasingly human in appearance and
personality. The humanizing of Santa Claus has undoubtedly
been furthered by the career of the professional Santa Claus
and by the mortal attributes given him in numerous literary
works.

Miracle on 34th Street provides a very modern setting for
the tale of the traditional figure of Santa Claus. It also uses
psychiatry, courtroom hearings, and romance, and places
much of its action in the pre-Christmas shopping season. In
spite of this milieu, the spirit of Christmas is potent enough
to convert even profit-making rivalry into mutual aid. The
popularity of the theme suggests its fundamental appeal.

The story will probably have little effect on Christmas
beliefs and lore because it was contrived chiefly to amuse
and interest. Nevertheless, *Miracle on 34th Street* is exceptional because it meets the issue of adult doubts about human
good will and generosity in a real world, not one of childish
fancy. Though the story fails to create new figures or to add
original motifs to Christmas lore, it proves, nevertheless, that
popular art can probe skillfully into the values and com-
plexities of the American Christmas.

Christmas Plays

Christmas is a favorite subject in another variety of popular
art. This is the short play, usually limited to one act, which
can be performed by groups of amateur actors and requires
little scenery or equipment. Its popularity increased suddenly
about 1900, and it has retained public favor to the present.

Church, school, and civic groups throughout the country produce these plays, which contribute substantially to perpetuating the traditional popularity of Christmas. They also dramatize its significance by offering solutions to contemporary problems achieved through the magic of the "Christmas spirit." In this respect the modern Christmas play resembles the Miracle plays of medieval Europe and England. However, the contemporary dramas are not folk art, nor are they concerned exclusively with religious themes. They are written and published with a mass market in view, and offer standardized treatments of stereotyped human situations. On this basis they may be classified as popular art.

An examination of fifty recent Christmas plays, published by two leading firms, throws light on their character and themes.[13] Sixteen were laid in ancient Bethlehem, five in medieval Europe, twenty-three in contemporary United States, and six elsewhere. Thus both the traditional and the modern are recognized in the locales of the plays. It should be added that none of the plays occurred in the far North or in surroundings associated with Santa Claus.

When the main themes or lessons of the fifty plays were classified, traditional ones dominated: of the total number of plays forty-three were devoted to narratives concerning the Nativity, or taught that the "Christmas spirit" caused people to behave in an ethical manner or induced self-sacrifice which was invariably rewarded at Christmas. Only seven plays could not be grouped under one of the above themes. A few dealt with the motif of acquisitiveness and overemphasis on gift exchanging, while one attempted to solve the problem of anti-Semitism by relating it to implications of the Nativity. Generally, they were overwhelmingly concerned with conventional religious and moral themes. In this respect, plays differ from other kinds of popular Christmas art.

So far as characters of the plays are concerned, they consisted mostly of family members—with emphasis on children

—neighbors, the poor, and the unfortunate. Only one play in the group involved the figure of Santa Claus. Apparently this type of popular art deals chiefly with the religious aspect of Christmas and teaches Christian precepts. The frequency with which these Christmas dramas are produced, and their involvement of children either as actors or as spectators, probably contribute not a little to transmitting some familiarity with the Nativity to each generation.

However, it is chiefly the social circumstances under which these plays are given that generate their influence on Christmas. As the holiday period approaches, a sense of excitement and urgency seizes most communities, and affects children in particular. Children usually participate in plays as members of distinct age and interest groups, thus causing them to associate the occasion with their peer groups. In later years Christmas is remembered as a time when a particular schoolroom, club, or other organized unit participated collectively in public holiday activities.

In addition, Christmas plays offer an opportunity for entire families to take part in community activities. They do so if only as members of an audience. Parents usually attend Christmas plays, operettas, and pageants at the behest of their children and to see them appear in public. This provides both generations with a sense of joint participation in an important occasion, strengthens family ties and, by implication, associates Christmas with kinship as well as with the peer group. Thus Christmas plays are important in perpetuating the festival in American culture by integrating it with significant social experiences in the lives both of parents and of children.

"Popular" Christmas Music

A great deal of popular music about Christmas has been written recently, and Tin Pan Alley turns out new holiday tunes each year. Few of these catch the public fancy or add much to the festival, though they range from Irving Berlin's "White Christmas" (1942) to Spike Jones's "All I Want for Christmas" (is my two front teeth) (1947) and "I Saw Mommy Kissing Santa Claus," by Tommie Connor (1952). However, Berlin's song is exceptional, has gained wide popularity, and promises to become a fixture in the holiday. Spike Jones's piece continues to attract attention as an amusing travesty on conventional Christmas songs, but it is not likely to endure.

With the exception of "White Christmas" and Marks's "Rudolph the Red-Nosed Reindeer," popular Christmas music offers little that is new, either in subject or in melody. Nearly all examples of this type of music published in the past ten years elaborate only the traditional elements of Christmas lore. Thus, Santa Claus is a favorite topic in "Here Comes Santa Claus," by Autry and Haldeman, and in "Santa Claus Is Comin' to Town," by Gillespie and Coots. His reindeer also provide song writers with a topic, for example, "Thirty-Two Feet and Eight Little Tails," by Redmond, Cavanaugh, and Weldon. In addition, the Christmas tree is another favorite subject. This is apparent in "Christine the Christmas Tree," by Pinterally, Drake, and Shirl, and in "The Christmas Tree Angel," by Scholl and Jerome. These titles are representative of Christmas subjects in recent popular songs.

As far as music is concerned, these songs have little to offer to enhance Christmas except the novelty of a different tune. They use rocking rhythms to suggest the motion of a sleigh and chromatic melodies to create a nostalgic mood. "Here Comes Santa Claus" is an example of the first technique and "White Christmas" of the second. Some recent popular Christmas tunes are thinly disguised variations of the old-fashioned "Jingle Bells." These add little to the musical resources of the occasion.

However, the words in a few of these songs throw light on contemporary attitudes toward the festival. For instance,

"Here Comes Santa Claus" admonishes children to give thanks to the Lord because Santa Claus is coming to visit them. This advice is accompanied by the equalitarian assurance that Santa Claus doesn't care if they are rich or poor, for he will love them just the same. The linking of the Christian deity with the pagan gift bringer is an example of how popular art cultivates public confusion about the meaning of Christmas. In general, popular Christmas songs exploit only a few folk subjects and seldom mention the Nativity, charity, family ties, or human brotherhood. This is surprising in view of the prominence of these values in the festival.

It probably reflects the fact that most music of this type is written to appeal to children rather than to adults. The young are attracted by words and music which symbolize Christmas gifts, joy, and excitement rather than by its spiritual and humanitarian aspects. This fits in with the American belief that "Christmas is for the children," and inclines parents to supply them with music of their choice. It results in neglect of the more traditional melodies. In addition, adults cannot sponsor familiarity with holiday folk music in successful competition with the popular Christmas tunes children hear on commercial radio programs.

The mass media of entertainment place a heavy premium on novelty, and this lures song writers to grind out new Christmas songs each year. If their tunes are popular for even a few weeks, the financial rewards from radio, recordings, and sheet music are substantial. This ensures a constant supply of new Christmas songs, which seem about to displace the older, traditional ones. This will come about in spite of continuing affection for old carols and songs such as "Silent Night," "O Little Town of Bethlehem," and "Good King Wenceslas," which have a folk as well as a religious character. Though these songs continue to appear on radio programs, they are usually played or sung by professional musicians. In time this will diminish public familiarity with the old tunes, and the popular will slowly displace the traditional in Christmas music. However, churches and other ecclesiastical organizations which use only religious music at Christmas will aid in preserving old songs and melodies from extinction.

The influence of popular music on Christmas resembles that of most other types of popular art. It emphasizes the folk aspects of the occasion and tends to interpret Christmas in terms of gifts and gratification. An indirect consequence is neglect of the religious character of the occasion. Popular music also stresses the importance of children in the celebration, and mirrors the national concern and affection for the young. Thus it reflects contemporary American society in important respects and contributes to transforming the national festival.

Christmas Cards

The extension of the Christmas-card custom to nearly all social groups in the United States has provided a mass market for another kind of popular Christmas art. Today a number of firms supply perhaps a billion and a half Christmas greeting cards to an eager public each year.[14] Most of these cards provide stereotyped portrayals of Christmas which are designed primarily for large sales. They include reproductions of famous Nativity paintings and the numerous familiar designs of the secular celebration.

Contemporary American Christmas cards fall into two major types: the traditional and the modern. Within each of these types certain varieties appear. Thus the traditional cards divide fairly readily into religious and folk categories. The former uses designs depicting the Nativity, the journey of the Wise Men, shepherds and their flocks, the Star of Bethlehem, angels, cherubs, and churches. The latter employs the figure of Santa Claus, candles, family dinner scenes, the

Christmas tree, domestic animals, children, birds, vegetation, wintry scenes, houses, barns, coaches, and decorations. The message of the religious card usually centers about the Nativity, while those on the secular or folk card simply express "good wishes" for the Christmas and New Year season.

The modern Christmas card has several recognizable varieties. The first one uses traditional figures—religious and folk —but caricatures them. Thus, figures of angels are made to resemble those of humans, cherubs are converted into children, and Santa Claus is portrayed in line drawings that contribute psychiatric overtones to the jolly gift bringer. Steinberg's drawings, "Santa Claus Skating" and "Santa on a Monument," [15] are examples of the last-named type of treatment. They signify acceptance of Christmas but not of the traditional card, and are used most frequently by the intellectual and professional classes. Some persons refuse to send cards of the traditional type and welcome ones that recognize Christmas in terms of humor and irony.

A second variety is the card which lacks any elements of design related to Christmas either in its religious or in its folk aspects. Such cards frequently carry reproductions of scenes or paintings from distant countries, of ships at sea or of animals. This type recognizes Christmas only through a message or salutation on the card. Persons sending this greeting symbol often do so in a conscious effort to avoid the sentimentality of the traditional card, or perhaps as a sign of rebellion against some aspects of the celebration. This variety also affords some possibility of originality and distinction in observing the custom.

A third variety of the modern card carries a picture of a family group and is often homemade. It emphasizes the family-centered character of Christmas and is most likely to be used when children are in the home. It ignores alike the Nativity and Santa Claus in favor of the domestic significance of the occasion.

Another interesting example of the modern card uses both its design and message to propagandize for special causes. Thus in recent years special cards have been designed for Negroes. Though these are conventional in figures and scenes, both the children and the adults portrayed have dark skin and kinky hair.[16] This type of card was manufactured specifically for Negroes who seek a closer identification of Christmas imagery with their own race. In addition, those interested in reducing racial or religious prejudice have devised Christmas cards which depict members of different social groups celebrating the festival of Christmas in a spirit of equality and brotherhood.[17] It is apparent that the different types and varieties of Christmas cards reflect both traditional and contemporary forces in the festival.

The custom of sending greeting cards at Christmas has spread steadily since it began in the late 1870's. It has become a communication device used by millions of Americans each year to reaffirm significant personal and social relationships. For this reason care is exercised in maintaining one's Christmas card list and in selecting appropriate cards for different persons. In some social circles it is said to be as important *not* to send cards to some persons as it is essential to send them to others.[18]

It is also interesting that Jews find that the Christmas-card custom involves them in conflicts between religious loyalty and community participation. As a token of the Nativity observance, the religious Christmas card is unacceptable to the orthodox Jew, yet the custom has a secular aspect as well. Therefore Jews vary in their attitude toward the custom. Some do not send Christmas cards at all, while others send them only to gentiles, and avoid cards with Christian imagery.

In recent years many business firms, hotels, and institutions have adopted the Christmas-card custom in the effort to cultivate good will and as a form of advertising. This has increased the tendency to regard the greeting card as a device calculated "to win friends and influence people" rather than as a spontaneous expression of good will at Christmas. However, the not inconsiderable emotional resources generated by Christmas will probably ensure the continued use of the greeting card in spite of attacks of doubt and suspicion.

Christmas Comic Books

Through yet another medium—the comic book—popular art exploits Christmas and influences children's understanding of the occasion. This innovation has attained great popularity among the younger age groups because these inexpensive (10- and 25-cent) paper-covered books dramatize a variety of topics in pictures which are accompanied by a narrative in words. They portray animals and people as alike in many respects. Thus creatures such as bears, deer, wolves, woodchucks, mice, and birds speak, think, feel, and act like human beings. This is not without precedent, but it is peculiarly effective in comic books. The plots are simple and deal chiefly with adventures and preach moral maxims that are easily grasped. American children have long been familiar with this type of entertainment in newspaper "funnies."

Comic books concentrate on Santa Claus's preparation for his annual trip and the actual delivery of presents. They carry such titles as "Santa Claus Funnies," "The Santa Claus Parade," and "Holiday Comics." Others, such as "Bugs Bunny's Christmas Funnies" and "The Newest Adventures of Rudolph the Red-Nosed Reindeer," make their respective characters the central figures in numerous stories but anchor them to Santa Claus. Comic books also contain non-Christmas stories in pictures and in print, puzzles, music, and words to Christmas songs. They provide a variety of entertainment for children from six to twelve in particular.

Comic books uniformly stress the folk-secular aspects of

Christmas and exploit the role of Santa Claus in particular. Little is said of the Nativity or of familial attributes of the celebration. Emphasis on charity, kindness, and generosity is rare in the Christmas comic books. This is in striking contrast to the usual newspaper comics, which on December 24th or 25th devote each strip to expressing Christmas good wishes or depict acts of seasonal kindness. The plots of the comic books frequently revolve about the hazards that beset Santa Claus as he prepares to make his famous annual visit.

Stock characters in comic books are Santa Claus and his helpers, who may be elves, children, or animals. Occasionally figures combining the physical appearance of both angels and good fairies introduce a semireligious note into the stories which is another instance of popular art confusing public understanding of Christmas symbols.

Perhaps the most important influence comic books will exert on Christmas will be to diminish the influence of parents in familiarizing their children with holiday lore. Because simple illustrated stories about Christmas are now available at low cost, children are likely to gain comprehension of it increasingly from each other. Each age group will tend to learn from the next older one and to spread such knowledge laterally to its members. This may well provide both an easier introduction to the figure of Santa Claus, for instance, and reduce shock when disillusionment comes. Beyond this, comic books will increase the influence of folk and secular forces in Christmas, as is true of most kinds of popular art.

Art and Christmas

The Christmas celebration has been preserved and enriched by both "fine" and folk art. Thus the music, painting, and stories concerning the Nativity have done much to keep alive the spiritual character of this observance for centuries.

These art products survived Puritan hostility and contributed to the nineteenth century renascence of Christmas observance. Similarly, Nast's pictures of Santa Claus and Moore's poem about his "visit" have embodied and preserved important folk aspects of the celebration.

However, with the exception of plays, contemporary popular art has ignored the religious aspect of Christmas and has added little to its folk imagery. To date, Rudolph the Red-Nosed Reindeer is the only figure approaching originality to appear in popular Christmas art. It seems unlikely that this type of art will add much of enduring value to the cultural resources of Christmas. Popular art seems to be "outer directed" rather than "inner directed," as evinced by the fact that its themes and forms are contrived to please the contemporary public rather than to offer original interpretations of Christmas experiences.[19] This reflects its commercial character and suggests limits to its future development. In the main, popular Christmas art tends to secularize the occasion while traditional fine art preserves its religious significance.

At present, though modern Christmas art mirrors the presence of both religious and secular influences in the annual festival, it has not decisively affected its character. The reason is that the same traditional forms and meanings are exploited each Christmas, and little effort is made to interpret the changing significance of the occasion through new artistic media.

Nevertheless, it is to be hoped that artists will find Christmas worthy of serious reflection and interpretation because few Americans are unmoved by its cultural significance or by their personal involvement in the celebration. It embodies not only spiritual beliefs but also familial implications and the ideal of human brotherhood. These are themes which should challenge artists to interpret Christmas both in the traditional idioms and in new ways designed to grasp the contemporary meaning of the festival.

CHAPTER VI.

The Cult of Christmas

A general thesis of this book is that the American Christmas crystallized as a national festival during the latter part of the nineteenth century and, once established, has evinced a degree of autonomy, yet has remained responsive to dominant currents of American life. Thus it is no longer devoted exclusively to celebrating the Nativity nor to reviving traditional folk customs or beliefs on December 25th. Instead, a number of active forces in American life have been incorporated into the festival, and it has developed some new and distinctive traits during the present century. What is the result of this transformation?

There is good reason to believe that Christmas has become a diffuse, popular cult which annually involves a large part of the American population in its activities. Significantly, though the date for its ceremonies is fixed in commemoration of the Nativity, the national festival derives much of its vigor from other sources. Thus Christmas is also nourished by the ties of family life, by affection for children, by a willingness to aid the needy, and even by the profit-seeking activities of modern business. The main rites of the cult are found in the midnight Mass of December 24th, the church service on Christmas Sunday, the family tree and dinner, Christmas shopping, gift giving, charity, Santa Claus's visit and the Christmas-card custom. Even the holiday greeting "Merry Christmas" can be seen as a kind of ceremonial utterance. These activities are intended somehow to banish anxiety, to enhance the present, and to secure the future.

Membership in the cult of Christmas is open to all who comply with its external forms, especially those which symbolize generosity, family solidarity, affection for children, and sympathy for the unfortunate. This makes it possible for non-Christians to participate in its folk and secular aspects even if they do not accept its religious significance. It is also possible to ignore or slight the annual celebration, but this is always done at some cost to one's communal feelings.

Christmas and the Midwinter Cycle

There are indications that Christmas has regained its former seasonal character instead of being restricted to one or two days. Of course, the religious aspect of the occasion has always embraced an extended period, but this was not true of the folk celebration in nineteenth century United States. However, under the stimulus of modern commercial exploitation and planned welfare campaigns at Christmas, this traditional aspect has reappeared. It indicates an important change which links Christmas to adjacent holidays.

It is evident today that not only the religious but also the secular activities of the festival follow a regular course each year. This sequence is a part of a midwinter cycle of activities which begins with Thanksgiving and ends at New Year or on January 6th. Christmas exerts influence on these celebrations and is affected by them to some degree. Its articulation with these other occasions sustains a high level of excitement and contributes to the social effectiveness of the entire period.

Thanksgiving falls on the last Thursday of each November. In some respects it marks the end of fall and the beginning of winter, though this characterization does not hold true in all parts of the United States. This holiday resembles the harvest festivals of agrarian societies, and had its American origins in a similar historical context. However, it has lost its bucolic significance in a day of efficient food preservation and has become simply an occasion warranting a holiday from work or school and an elaborate family dinner. Furthermore, it encourages the dignified expression of patriotism in official proclamations of the President and the governors of the various states. These statements usually recite the blessings of the nation and attribute them to the favor of the Almighty.

During the eighteenth and most of the nineteenth century, Thanksgiving was more popular than Christmas in New England.[1] Even though this situation has changed, "Turkey Day" is still observed with enthusiasm in all parts of the country. It calls for a ceremonial meal resembling one eaten by the Pilgrims after they survived the first winter on this continent. Thus the observance hints at ancestor worship, and provides a fitting introduction to Christmas—a festival of the family, church, and community.

The Christmas rites, both religious and folk, occur in a series of stages. These may be termed preparation, climax, and aftermath. The first covers the period December 1st to 23rd, the second, December 24th and 25th, and the third, December 26th to January 6th. This sequence marks the progression of the festival from its inception to its completion. Each period exhibits different functions.

The first stage prepares celebrants psychologically to take part in the climactic rites which occur on December 24th and 25th. It is a "warming up" period which encourages participants to "get the Christmas spirit" in preparation for the culmination of the festival. Devout Christians are expected to ready themselves for observing the Nativity by attending Advent services, by fasting, self-denial, and charity. This involves interaction with other persons of like beliefs, participation in the traditional Christmas liturgy, and the exaltation of spiritual values over all others. Frequently, manger scenes appear on the lawns of churches and houses, symbolizing the Christian character of the occasion. The rites of this preparatory period provide psychological power which propels the festival toward its climax.

During the introductory stage those who participate in the folk aspect of Christmas buy presents, cards, and food, give to charity, and go to parties and plays. They also decorate their homes and obtain a tree. Most of these activities are likely to increase social contacts, to stimulate good will, and intensify the sense of anticipation.

If the first period exhibits an atmosphere of anticipation, the second one asserts a mood of fulfillment. The festival reaches its climax on December 24th and 25th. The religious observance culminates in the midnight Mass of the Roman Catholic Church on Christmas Eve and in the Christmas Sunday services of Protestant denominations. Many families decorate their trees on the evening of December 24th and distribute presents on the following morning. In addition they eat the traditional holiday dinner—which usually includes turkey—on December 25th.

Both religious and domestic rites have important effects on this stage of the festival because they bring people together under circumstances where they stimulate one another, express common feelings, share experiences, and reanimate their faith in one another. This tends to reinforce social unity, and may also provide individual satisfactions in terms of enhanced self-esteem and physical gratification. Candor requires recognition that the Christmas rites do not have these results in all instances. However, their persistence year after year suggests that most groups find them rewarding.

The family celebration expresses and emphasizes the idea of unity during the climax stage. This is apparent in several ways. For example, erecting and decorating the Christmas tree involves all members of the family, even though one or two may take the lead in this activity. It is understood that the tree belongs to the entire family rather than to a single member. In addition, gift distribution symbolizes unity in that every person present at a family gathering must receive something as a token of inclusion in the group.[2] There is also a common feeling that gifts should be approximately equal in number and value, and they are seldom given out until every member of the family is present. These provisions often include visitors, servants, and even animals. The Christmas dinner also symbolizes the unity of those related by descent and marriage as they engage in a kind of "alimentary communion." This may produce greater family unity, as well as indigestion.

The second stage is also distinguished by public ceremonial acts. These include the President's annual message to the public, carol singing on the lawn of the White House, Christmas-morning religious services in outdoor places of worship, and Christmas programs on radio and television. In some parts of the country, custom still permits celebrants to shoot guns and explode firecrackers during the holiday. These acts contribute to a general feeling of release, happiness, and fulfillment, and most persons radiate friendliness and good will at this high point of the celebration.

An interesting indication of the ritual character of the first and second stages of the Christmas festival is found in their prohibitions. Because the festival is one of brotherhood and peace, informal though powerful interdictions against aggressiveness or punitive acts appear during both periods. This is particularly strong in families and other intimate groups.

Moreover, criminal courts seldom try cases just before or during the holiday, and prisoners are often pardoned or paroled "in time for Christmas." There is also a general disapproval of physical violence, and those inclined to fight or quarrel are urged to wait "until Christmas is over."

As might be expected, these stages of Christmas also manifest a prohibition against selfishness and greed which finds its positive expression in the duty of generosity and charity. It should be noted that the Roman Catholic Church prescribes a fast for this time, and it is also possible that a mild interdiction against overeating generally prevails during the preparatory period. In fact, most persons reserve their holiday feasting for the dinner on Christmas Day.

Though there is no formal taboo on sexual relations during the second stage of Christmas, it is doubtful if there is much increase in erotic activity at this time. An intensified interest in sex might be expected because of the general atmosphere of relaxation and indulgence and the considerable increase in social stimulation. However, only the imputed excesses of "office parties" suggest that this occurs. Probably a festival which emphasizes family unity does so at the expense of individual interest in sexual activity.

During the days between December 26th and January 6th, the festival moves to its conclusion. After December 26th, holiday enjoyment continues, but at a slower pace. People make visits, enjoy their gifts, remove tree decorations, and plan parties and dinners for New Year's Eve. Christmas music and plays usually disappear from radio and television programs. Gifts may be exchanged for more desirable ones at some stores, and "returns" of Christmas purchases run high the first few days after December 25th.[3] A sense of completion and letdown pervades the aftermath period, revealed in a tendency to wax philosophical or flippant in evaluating Christmas and to be "glad that it's over."

The party on December 31st, New Year's Eve, is an interesting episode in the seasonal cycle. Friends, acquaintances, and neighbors gather in homes, and various social groups have parties at clubs or public places. Unlike the Christmas dinner, which includes children and emphasizes family and generation unity, the New Year's Eve party is limited to adults. It frequently involves drinking, music, dancing, various degrees of amatory license, pranks, noisemaking, and general merriment. The high point of the occasion is midnight, which marks the end of the old year and the beginning of the new one. At this juncture, couples kiss, toasts are offered to the New Year, and many kinds of noise ensue. These acts express a "hail and farewell" mood. Pictures portraying this termination rite employ the figure of Father Time and a young child to symbolize the end of the old and the beginning of the new year. It seems more than coincidental that the key symbols of both the Nativity and the New Year are children.

The New Year's Eve party offers opportunity for indulging in kinds of behavior not approved either in the Nativity observance or in the domestic Christmas. Nevertheless, the desire to engage in such activity apparently persists widely, and the possibilities of the evening of December 31st are exploited freely. Cartoons appearing on January 1st reflect the parties held on New Year's Eve by depicting a conventional middle-aged male suffering from a hangover and forced to listen to his wife's catalogue of his excesses of the previous evening. This stereotype has become a fixture in the aftermath of the evening's celebration.

The New Year's party suggests ambivalence about the annual round. That is, it not only promotes seasonal conviviality, but many persons also exhibit overtones of satisfaction that the period—especially Christmas—is over and can be forgotten for many months. This underscores the view that it is a time of obligations, anxieties and tensions, as well as one of happiness and social communion.[4] Many persons are glad to put both Christmas and the old year behind them.

Some time after New Year's Day most families put away their Christmas decorations and remove the tree from the house. In large cities this poses serious problems for sanitation departments, which must dispose of thousands of trees. Wreaths and exterior decorations are the last mementoes of Christmas to disappear, and some families retain theirs even after Epiphany. Though the festivities of Christmas are over, the obligations of the cult remain: there are "thank you" letters to be written, bills to be paid, experiences to be treasured or forgotten, and perhaps tentative plans made for the next Christmas. The lure of post-Christmas sales even leads some persons to buy presents for the next celebration. This round continues each year, and indicates the continuing vitality of the Christmas cult.

To Each His Own

The importance of Christmas is not due to chance nor to any intrinsic magic of the occasion, as many persons fondly believe. Rather, its popularity, psychological force, and "spirit" reflect the recurring success of countless persons in gratifying desires and in satisfying pressing emotional needs through its rites and customs. In addition, it embodies basic social values which may account for its persistence, even in the face of considerable hostility at certain periods in history. One may be sure that if Christmas did not make possible the realization of individual satisfactions and collective values, some other holiday would be used to achieve these ends. In this connection it is pertinent to remember that Thanksgiving surpassed Christmas in popularity in New England well into the nineteenth century.

Most persons experience the common rewards of Christmas, and also find it a source of unique individual satisfactions.

Chief among these is the sharp break it provides with daily routines, particularly occupational ones. This has come to be so important that a holiday from work at Christmas is considered to be almost a "right," and persons who must work on December 25th are viewed with great sympathy. Those who do so for unselfish ends are greatly admired. For instance, a reviewer of the diaries of the late James Forrestal, Secretary of the Navy and later of Defense, cited the fact that Forrestal worked late at his desk one Christmas Day as convincing proof of his patriotism and devotion to the national welfare.[5]

However, the insistence on a Christmas holiday seems to reflect chiefly a wish to escape from unsatisfactory job situations rather than a desire to celebrate the occasion with appropriate rites. This interpretation is supported by the impression that vacations appear to be most highly prized by persons who are employed at routinized tasks, as in the case of factory and office workers. On the other hand, professional persons, farmers, artists, and scientists who enjoy more flexible and rewarding types of work are less insistent concerning the necessity of a respite. Thus some persons attach unique importance to the Christmas holiday chiefly because it provides an escape from their jobs. Apparently this zeal for vacations became pronounced after the appearance of large numbers of employees in clerical and industrial occupations. Since the beginning of the present century, it has spread to nearly all types of employment.

Christmas also provides other important gratifications of both a physical and emotional sort. For instance, most persons look forward to unusual indulgence in holiday food and drink, and eating and drinking to excess is considered a virtue at this one time of the year. Such seasonal permissiveness pleases those who "live to eat" and reassures those who must diet or reduce. Furthermore, most persons obtain considerable satisfaction from receipt of Christmas presents and cards, whether these are interpreted as proof of their social importance or evidence of personal affection.

Another important benefit associated with Christmas is the seasonal increase in affection, kindness, and friendliness, paralleled by a decline in hostility and competitiveness. During the festival—especially the climax stage—enemies tend to avoid or postpone quarrels, strangers speak to one another readily, adults are permissive to children, and family members feel more closely drawn together. Also, athletic contests and sports events involving competitive struggle are generally avoided during the second stage of Christmas.[6] In addition, the police are tolerant of some minor offenses, and even judges are known to be lenient just before December 25th. In fact, a blanket of good will covers most conventional activity during the immediate holiday period.

However, it should not be thought that the above satisfactions of Christmas are uniform among all Americans. Even some of those who observe Christmas rites are lukewarm in their enthusiasm, and others dislike the occasion chiefly because it interrupts their daily routines. There are also those who obtain little satisfaction from the annual exchange of gifts and regret the after-effects of holiday feasting. Probably some persons dislike the domestic celebration because they find themselves, against their wills, being drawn more closely into the kinship orbit.

Families with members in the armed forces may find that Christmas is a painful time because it high-lights the uncertainties of the future where loved ones are concerned. Inevitably the festival provokes deep emotional conflict under such circumstances. Furthermore, persons who experience unhappiness or tragedy at a particular Christmas, such as death of family members, serious illness, or other misfortune, may discover that successive celebrations awaken poignant memories.

Christmas and Social Values

These considerations suggest that Christmas must be supported by quite basic values in order to over-ride its possible negative implications. It appears that the main ones are brotherhood and family life. Both are traditional in Western civilization and are widely accepted in the Christian, Judaic, or humanistic traditions. However, they are in evident conflict with other powerful social values such as nationalism, individualism, and success. As a result, daily life in contemporary United States exhibits frequent neglect of brotherly love and domestic life.

Nevertheless, these values have great strength and are integral parts of American culture. As such, they demand renewal, and each Christmas millions of Americans reaffirm their belief in brotherhood and family life. Quite often they also attempt to expiate their neglect of these during the previous months. This interpretation throws light on the almost frenzied efforts at Christmas charity and explains some of the compulsiveness behind family gatherings, messages, gifts, and cards.

There can be no doubt about the fundamental importance of Christianity in the American Christmas cult, particularly in relation to the inculcation and maintainence of its basic social values. Of course, the very name of the festival refers to the Mass of Christ, and for centuries the observance has formally commemorated His birth. Moreover, the Nativity account is replete with indirect affirmations of family life and brotherhood, and the Christian Church has generally thrown the weight of its influence to the support of these social values.

However, it must also be recognized that the national Christmas cult draws strength from other than Christian sources, even where brotherhood and family life are concerned. Though these values are basic in Christian teachings, they have also appeared in other religions and have developed a considerable degree of autonomy. Today they are widely supported by non-Christian religious groups as well as by persons without definite religious convictions.

In addition, the lore and customs of the folk celebration have done much to popularize the festival. In fact, at times these influences seem to overshadow its religious and spiritual ones. Moreover, it is quite possible that the folk-secular aspects of the Christmas cult might persist even if the Nativity commemoration should disappear. This opinion reflects the conviction that family solidarity, charitable sentiments, and gift exchanging at Christmas have acquired impressive social and psychological significance in their own right. Furthermore, many business groups have acquired an important financial stake in the festival and can be counted on to exercise diligence and ingenuity to perpetuate their interest. Thus both religious and secular factors support the national Christmas cult.

In this connection the popularity of the office party, as well as the criticism directed against it, demonstrates the dual influences at work in Christmas. Some of these parties are quite conventional and simply use the occasion to express good will among those who work together. Others resemble the Saturnalian revels of the Romans. Recently an American magazine described this type of Christmas celebration:

On one night or another just before Christmas the lights burn late in many American business houses. The occasion is that great leveller, the office Christmas party, an antidote for formality which ranks between a few discreet cocktails and a free-for-all fight. Then all business barriers collapse; executives unbend; the office clown finds a sympathetic audience. This is the only time the pretty file clerk gets kissed in public and the homely one gets kissed at all.[7]

This festivity of the urban business world has acquired considerable popularity, and the censured type of party appears to be on the increase. Perhaps this is because it provides a break in work routines, temporarily banishes distinctions of rank in the office, furnishes alcohol, encourages singing and pranks and even tolerates amatory activity. It is completely secular and ignores the religious and familial character of Christmas.

In fact, critics of this kind of office party allege that it violates the sanctity of the Nativity observance and also endangers the moral values of family life.[8] They also assert that it causes automobile accidents because of drunken driving, and fear that it encourages improper behavior between the sexes. In addition, they charge that the office party prevents husbands and fathers from spending Christmas Eve with their wives and children, since it is frequently held on December 24th and lasts well into the evening.

Under a barrage of criticism from religious leaders, temperance societies, and even public officials, some firms have forbidden the office party. Others have banished alcohol from the celebration. This decision reflects unhappy experiences with previous parties as well as sensitivity to public condemnation. Thus, paradoxically, both the office party and the criticism it has aroused demonstrate the strength of religious and folk elements in the American Christmas.

Christmas as an American Symbol

Another powerful force which supports the American Christmas cult is the belief that it is a vital and unique symbol of our national life and culture. Significantly, this view prevails both in the United States and in other countries. This is especially true of the folk Christmas, which reflects American secular culture more extensively than does religious observance of the occasion. It has become so intimately identified with national life that adoption of the Santa Claus figure, the Christmas tree, and gift exchanging now demonstrate an important stage of acculturation for recent immigrants.[9] Americans also show a pronounced inclination to believe that Christmas, in some form, is celebrated by all peoples of the world. This is simply not true, and the belief clearly indicates an unconscious attempt to generalize from our own national festival.

Americans who are abroad at Christmas make efforts to reproduce the celebration according to their memories of previous ones held at home. Even American soldiers near battlefields have practiced the rite of Santa Claus's visit.[10] They improvised costumes and decorations and even distributed presents to front-line troops by airplanes. In addition, for many years the Quartermaster Corps of the American Army has made strenuous efforts to provide each soldier with the traditional turkey dinner on Christmas Day. During the war in Korea, the Communists attempted to capitalize on the emotional impact of the occasion by broadcasting Christmas-carol music to American troops as December 25th approached in the effort to make them homesick and less inclined to fight. These things emphasize the close identification of Christmas with the American way of life.

Within the United States a few national or cultural groups have resisted, somewhat self-consciously, the incursion of the American Christmas. The Pennsylvania Germans, Latin Americans of the Southwest, Greeks, and Scandinavians have been most energetic in their opposition and most successful in preserving their traditional Christmas festivals. Among these groups it is noticeable that religious and folk aspects of their celebrations are closely interwoven. This has given greater integration to their festivals and perhaps enabled them to resist pressure from the dominant American pattern. Nevertheless, it is probably only a matter of decades until these parochial celebrations lose their vitality and their forms disappear by attrition. This may occur by stages in which, at first, the two different Christmases will exist side by side; later they will merge or one will displace the other. Examples of such acculturation processes are to be found in the contemporary Southwest, where borrowing is taking place between the American and Spanish Christmases.[11]

A further proof of the national character of our festival is that other countries identify it with dominant traits of the United States. In particular, they consider Santa Claus to be an American figure. This has come about partly through the efforts of our business firms to exploit the occasion in other countries and by the presence of American "colonies" in many parts of the world. Above all, American soldiers fighting in World War II disseminated the folk Christmas. They gave parties for local children and introduced the figure of Santa Claus and the idea of Christmas gifts so effectively that the terms "American" and "Christmas" have become synonymous with the idea of bounty throughout the world.

Each country reacts to the American Christmas on its own terms. England accepted Santa Claus some time during the latter part of the nineteenth century and has adopted the American turkey for Christmas dinner very widely.[12] In addition, in very recent years, both the song and story of Rudolph the Red-Nosed Reindeer have become well known there. Puerto Rico, though an American possession, has a different cultural base and, until recently, celebrated Three Kings' Day on January 6th and paid little attention to Christmas. However, of late years its urban residents in middle- or upper-income groups have begun to celebrate the latter occasion and to introduce Santa Claus as the gift bringer. This sign of acculturation is exhibited particularly by economically successful persons on the island. It suggests a local identification of Christmas, material wealth, and American culture. A similar process is also occurring in urban centers in the Philippine Islands and Mexico.[13]

Though the folk Christmas was popular in Japan before

World War II, it was suppressed during the conflict. Recently, the celebration has been revived and has grown in public favor.[14] This can be attributed partly to the presence of American occupation forces in Japan and also to the dependence of the Japanese economy on American bounty. Under these circumstances the figure of the American Santa Claus, whose generosity knows no limits, is a likely one for the Japanese to adopt. They may cultivate it both for political and for material reasons.

Other countries have opposed parts or all of the American celebration. These range from Spain, which banned the use of the English word "Christmas" in Spanish newspapers in 1950, to Hungary, which began to discredit Santa Claus in 1951.[15] In Spain this action was taken because its powerful Catholic clergy consider Christmas folk customs essentially Protestant in nature. Under its present government Hungary followed the Communist "line" by deriding Santa Claus as a "tool of American capitalist interests." This recalls the earlier opposition of Soviet Russia to Christmas.[16] In addition, in 1941, a cultural organization in South Africa denounced Santa Claus as "a foreign importation unsuited to the ideals of Afrikanders."

The French in Canada are also suspicious of Santa Claus, and in 1947 a Catholic laymen's organization attacked him as a "neopagan custom" and "a farce that has lasted too long."[17] This is another proof that the Church is fighting to protect the religious significance of Christmas against secular encroachment. In France, too, the Catholic clergy has occasionally made hostile statements about Santa Claus, with the result that anticlerical groups, even including Communists, have defended him as a matter of political strategy.[18] There is no doubt that the French, as well as other Europeans, regard Santa Claus as an American symbol. This is true in spite of the fact that he developed from Dutch and German folklore and that France has a similar figure known as Père Noël.

The widespread identification of Christmas with the American way of life has added nationalism to Christian beliefs, brotherhood, and family ties as major forces tending to perpetuate the cult in the United States. In fact, this resemblance is striking if account is taken of the actual celebration rather than of its romanticized version. Thus, in spite of its formal dominance by Christianity, the festival reflects pagan beliefs and customs in a manner which recalls the struggle waged by religious and secular forces for control of American life. Moreover, the contemporary Christmas reveals a great, if occasionally reluctant, devotion to family life that parallels rather closely the attitudes of Americans toward their immediate kin. Even Christmas charity exhibits that splendid mixture of generosity, calculation, and sentimentality so characteristic of beneficence in this country. In addition, the prominent influence of commercialism in the annual festival reminds one that this is a business civilization and that it has given hostages to the search for profits, to advertising and competition.

For these reasons a multitude of persons can find varied satisfactions in the Christmas cult. To some it offers abundant spiritual rewards, while others enjoy it chiefly as a means of renewing fraternal and family ties. On the other hand, many value Christmas chiefly for its material gratifications and resent its obligations. Finally, it must not be forgotten that there are those who dislike the celebration. Thus each person discovers the meaning of Christmas for himself according to fortune and his needs.

This brings to a close the effort to trace the development of the American Christmas from colonial times to the present and to describe and assess its contemporary character and functions. The writer has tried to show how the past and the present, the religious and the secular, are fused in the pattern of the national festival so that it draws vitality from many and varied sources. This has given the celebration an appeal that often transcends the restrictions of belonging to certain age, sex, religious, and economic groups, and promotes a wider sense of human brotherhood.

At the same time it seems clear that the American Christmas shows the impress of our national culture and draws vigor from this identification. Specifically, it is linked closely to church, family, school, charity, and the prevailing economic system. These ties give it firm community support and assure its perpetuation for a long time to come. However, it is also necessary to recognize that the inevitable contradictions of a complex society and compelling community pressure to observe Christmas produce strains and tensions in many Americans at this "hallowed time." These facts cannot be ignored in any candid examination of the national festival. Finally, it appears quite certain that, though Christmas is a traditional festival, it is responsive to changes in American life and will develop new forms and meanings in future generations.

References and Notes

Chapter I. CHRISTMAS IN THE MAKING

[1] For bibliography see C. A. Miles, *Christmas in Ritual and Tradition*, and L. D. Johnston, "Classical Origins of Christmas Customs."

[2] K. L. Richards, *How Christmas Came to the Sunday-Schools*, p. 49.

[3] G. W. Curtis, "Christmas," *Harper's New Monthly Magazine*, 68:13, Dec., 1883.

[4] *Ibid.*, p. 10.

[5] *Ibid.*, p. 14.

[6] Richards, *op. cit.*, pp. 45 f.

[7] Curtis, *op. cit.*, p. 15.

[8] See the Diary of Cotton Mather, Pt. II, p. 146, entry for Dec. 30, 1711, *Massachusetts Historical Collections*, Vol. VIII.

[9] Richards, *op. cit.*, pp. 53 f.

[10] A. E. Brown, "The Ups and Downs of Christmas in New England," *New England Magazine*, 29:483, 1903.

[11] W. W. Manross, *The Episcopal Church, 1800–1840*, p. 178.

[12] Richards, *op. cit.*, p. 71.

[13] *Ibid.*, pp. 142 f.

[14] *Ibid.*, p. 77.

[15] *Ibid.*, p. 128.

[16] F. A. Collins, article in the *New York Times*, Dec. 25, 1921, VII, 2:7.

[17] Hartford *Daily Courant*, Dec. 22, 1834.

[18] Richards, *op. cit.*, p. 95.

[19] W. W. Sweet, *Chicago Theological Seminary Register*, 22:14, Nov., 1932.

[20] Richards, *op. cit.*, p. 195. This was foreshadowed earlier in an article on holidays which appeared in the *North American Review*, 84:344 f., 1857 (anonymous).

[21] Richards, *op. cit.*, pp. 51 f.

[22] John Esten Cooke, "Christmas Time in Old Virginia," *Magazine of American History*, 10:451, Dec., 1883.

[23] J. E. Wright and D. S. Corbett, *Pioneer Life in Western Pennsylvania*, p. 97.

[24] Martha J. Lamb, "Christmas Season in Dutch New York," *Magazine of American History*, 10:472, July–Dec., 1883.

[25] *Publications of the Pennsylvania German Folklore Society*, 6:13–14, 1941.

[26] Arthur M. Sowder, "Christmas Trees—The Tradition," in *Trees—The Yearbook of Agriculture, 1949* (Washington, D.C., United States Government Printing Office), p. 245.

[27] Frederic Klees, *The Pennsylvania Dutch*, pp. 347 ff.

[28] G. G. Johnson, *Ante-Bellum North Carolina*, pp. 552 f; see also "Christmas in Virginia Before the War," by Florence W. Lee, in the *Southern Workman*, Vol. 38, No. 12, Dec., 1908, pp. 687 ff.

[29] B. L. Heilbron, "Christmas and New Year's on the Frontier," *Minnesota History*, Vol. 16, No. 4, Dec., 1935, pp. 380 f.

[30] W. P. Webb, "Christmas and New Year in Texas," *Southwestern Historical Quarterly*, 44:365, July, 1940–April, 1941.

[31] W. H. Brewer, *Up and Down California in 1860–1864*, pp. 359 f.

[32] Editorial comment in *Brother Jonathan*, Dec. 24, 1842, p. 494.

[33] Cited by W. W. Watt in "Christmas, 1943—A Dickens Centenary," *Saturday Review of Literature*, 26:18, Dec. 4, 1943.

[34] André Maurois, *Dickens*, p. 3.

[35] See Edmund Wilson, "Dickens—The Two Scrooges," in *The Wound and the Bow*, and T. A. Jackson, *Charles Dickens: The Progress of a Radical*, pp. 285 ff.

[36] Support for this interpretation is found in *The Rise of the Common Man, 1830–1850*, by C. R. Fish, and in *The Emergence of Modern America, 1865–1878*, by Allan Nevins.

[37] Watt, *op. cit.*, p. 18.

[38] "American Holidays," *Saturday Review*, 62:18, July 3, 1886; see also *New York Daily Tribune*, Dec. 26, 1900.

³⁹ E. D. Chase, *The Romance of Greeting Cards*, p. 21.

⁴⁰ See "A Century of Christmas Cards," *American Home*, Dec., 1946, reproductions, pp. 16–18. Mr. Walker Nettleton, of Guilford, Conn., has a collection of Prang cards in his Industrial Museum.

⁴¹ *Harper's Weekly*, Dec. 26, 1863, pp. 824–25; Dec. 31, 1864, pp. 840–41; Dec. 29, 1866, pp. 824–25.

⁴² Richards, *op. cit.*, p. 157.

Chapter II. THE SOCIAL ROLE OF SANTA CLAUS

¹ Karl Meissen, "Nikolauskult und Nikolausbrauch im Abendlande," Heft 9–12, *Forschungen zur Volkskunde*, 1931; C. Catherine van de Graft, "Sinterklaas, Goedheilig Man," *Haagsch Maanblad*, Vol. 8, No. 12, Dec., 1927, pp. 626–636; A. de Groot, "Sint Nicolaas, Patroon van Liefde," Amsterdam, 1949; M. S. Crawford, "Life of Saint Nicholas," Ph.D. thesis, University of Pennsylvania, Philadelphia, 1923.

² A. J. Wall, Jr., "St. Nicholas at the Society," *Quarterly Bulletin of the New-York Historical Society*, 25:11, Jan., 1941.

³ *Ibid.*, p. 11.

⁴ L. D. Johnston, "Classical Origins of Christmas Customs," p. 94, Ph.D. thesis, University of Illinois, 1936.

⁵ P. A. Munch, *Norse Mythology*, pp. 46, 312.

⁶ Quoted in Wall, *op. cit.*, p. 12.

⁷ O. M. Spencer, "Christmas Throughout Christendom," *Harper's New Monthly Magazine*, 46:241–257, Dec., 1872.

⁸ Wall, *op. cit.*, p. 12.

⁹ Charles W. Jones, "Knickerbocker Santa Claus," *New-York Historical Society Quarterly* (in press, 1954).

¹⁰ Interesting discussions of this question appear in H. L. West, "Who Wrote ' 'Twas the Night Before Christmas'?" *The Bookman*, 52:300–305, Dec., 1920, and in H. W. Reynolds, "Editorial Notes on the Writings of Henry Livingston, Jr.," *Dutchess County Historical Society Yearbook*, 27:85–104, 1942.

¹¹ See the *New Mirror*, Dec. 30, 1943.

¹² Letter to writer, dated July 5, 1951; see also p. 70 of Vol. 6 of the *Scrapbook of the Writings of Frank Weitenkampf*, Art Division, the New York Public Library. In addition, see the 1837 Santa Claus portrait by R. Weir reproduced in the *Quarterly of the New-York Historical Society*, Oct., 1951.

[13] *Harper's Weekly*, Dec. 31, 1870, Vol. 14, pp. 849, 865, Christmas Supplement.

[14] *Ibid.*, Dec. 29, 1866, Vol. 10, pp. 824–825.

[15] *Ibid.*, Dec. 26, 1863, Vol. 7, pp. 824–826.

[16] Ednah Proctor Clarke, "The Revolt of Santa Claus," the *Ladies' Home Journal*, Dec., 1901, p. 19.

[17] See J. P. McCaskey, *Christmas in Song and Story*, and C. Johnson, *Songs Everyone Should Know*.

[18] See *The Home Book of Christmas*, by May Lamberton Becker, or *The Fireside Book of Christmas Stories*, by E. Wagenknecht.

[19] *Hartford Courant*, Dec. 26, 1947.

[20] *Ibid.*, Dec. 24, 1947.

[21] *Ibid.*, Dec. 17, 1950.

[22] *Ibid.*, Sept. 26, 1947.

[23] *Ibid.*, Oct. 14, 1947.

[24] *P.M.*, Dec. 24, 1947.

[25] *Outlook*, 112:66, Jan. 12, 1916.

[26] *New York Times*, Dec. 24, 1927, 16:3.

[27] *Time*, Dec. 18, 1950, p. 101. Copyright, Time, Inc., 1950.

[28] *New York Times*, Nov. 27, 1927, X, 10:2.

[29] *New Yorker*, Dec. 11, 1948, p. 26.

[30] *Hartford Courant*, Dec. 22, 1948.

[31] *New York Times*, Jan. 13, 1939, 4:2.

[32] *Ibid.*, Dec. 25, 1949, III, 2:3.

[33] *Business Week*, Nov. 20, 1937, pp. 40 f.

[34] See *Life*, Dec. 20, 1948, p. 64.

[35] *Collier's Weekly*, Dec. 15, 1923, pp. 10 f.

[36] Maybelle Manning, "You Can't Tell Some People There Is No Santa Claus," *American Home*, Dec., 1946, p. 25.

[37] *Ex parte Santa Claus*, an Unjudicial Judgment by Judge John H. Hatcher, Dec. 23, 1927, The Syllabus Service, Charleston, W. Va.

[38] *Ibid.*, p. 2.

[39] *New York Times*, Dec. 23, 1936, 19:3.

[40] "Santa Claus: A Psychograph," in E. Wagenknecht, *The Fireside Book of Christmas Stories*, p. 275.

[41] *New York Daily Tribune*, Dec. 28, 1903, 8:2.

[42] *New York Times*, Dec. 24, 1921, 4:2.

[43] *Ibid.*, Dec. 26, 1927, 30:5.

[44] *Time*, Aug. 21, 1950, p. 66. Copyright, Time, Inc., 1950.

[45] *Hartford Courant*, Dec. 26, 1949.

[46] *Ibid.*, Dec. 16, 1949.

[47] *New York Times*, Nov. 7, 1945, 25:6; Oct. 26, 1946, 6:8.

[48] See Catherine Mackenzie, "Is Santa a Menace?" *New York Times Magazine*, Dec. 23, 1945; also June Bingham, "Santa and the Debate Over Him Go On and On," *New York Times Magazine*, Dec. 18, 1949.

[49] A. Gesell, "Human Infancy and the Ontogenesis of Behavior," *American Scientist*, 37:547, 1949.

[50] Renzo Sereno, "Some Observations on the Santa Claus Custom," *Psychiatry*, Vol. 14, No. 4, Nov., 1951, pp. 387–396.

[51] *Ibid.*, p. 388.

[52] *Ibid.*, p. 389.

[53] "St. Monty," *New Yorker*, Dec. 19, 1942, p. 16; also Gesell, *op. cit.*, and innumerable stories and pictures appearing each Christmas involving children and Santa Claus.

[54] Robert Doane, *The Measurement of American Wealth*, pp. 42, 43.

[55] On this point see Talcott Parsons, "Age and Sex in the Social Structure of the United States," *American Sociological Review*, Oct., 1942, pp. 604–616; and Geoffrey Gorer, *The American People*, Chaps. 2, 3.

[56] Sereno, *op. cit.*, p. 392 n.

Chapter III. CHRISTMAS IN CHURCH, FAMILY, AND SCHOOL

[1] On this point the findings of J. H. Fichter, S.J., are interesting. See his *Southern Parish—Dynamics of a City Church*, pp. 155, 159.

[2] *New York Times*, Dec. 23, 1945, I:3.

[3] Compare the number of references to peace at Christmas during a war year with those made during a peaceful year. See the *New York Times* Index for 1945 and 1948.

[4] *Time*, Dec. 29, 1947, p. 34. Copyright, Time, Inc., 1947.

[5] H. Stroup, *The Jehovah's Witnesses*, p. 142.

[6] M. B. Eddy, *What Christmas Means to Me*, p. 45.

[7] Louis Witt, "The Jew Celebrates Christmas," *Christian Century*, Dec., 1939, p. 1497. Reprinted by permission.

[8] I. Lewy, "A Christmas Letter by a Jew," *Reconstructionist*, Dec. 24, 1948, p. 20.

[9] *Time*, Dec. 25, 1950, p. 28. Copyright, Time, Inc., 1950.

[10] *Ibid.*, Dec. 12, 1949, p. 53. Copyright, Time, Inc., 1949.

[11] *Hartford Courant,* July 23, 1949.

[12] John L. Thomas, S.J., "Religious Training in the Roman Catholic Family," *American Journal of Sociology,* Sept., 1951, p. 180.

[13] *Time,* Dec. 12, 1949, p. 53.

[14] A. Tille, *Yule and Christmas,* p. 123; see Chaps. 3, 4 in E. C. Rodgers, *Discussions of Holidays in the Later Middle Ages.*

[15] *Hartford Courant,* Dec. 25, 1948, p. 7.

[16] *New York Times,* Dec. 23, 1945, I:1.

[17] *Life,* Dec. 24, 1945, pp. 15 f.

[18] *Hartford Courant,* Dec. 22, 1948.

[19] *New York World Telegram,* March 6, 1951, p. 25. Copyright, United Features Syndicate, Inc., 1951.

[20] Channing Pollock, "There's Got to Be a Santa Claus," *Rotarian,* Dec., 1941, p. 7.

[21] Robin Williams, Jr., *American Society,* p. 69 n.

[22] J. H. S. Bossard and E. S. Boll, *Ritual in Family Living,* p. 77.

[23] *Ibid.,* pp. 178 f.

[24] *Ibid.,* p. 76.

[25] M. B. Sussman, "Family Continuity: A Study of Factors Which Affect Relationships Between Families at Generational Levels," Ph.D. thesis, Yale, 1951, pp. 94–95.

[26] L. Steffens, *Autobiography,* p. 20.

[27] J. Dollard, "The Life History in Community Studies," *American Sociological Review,* Vol. 3, No. 5, Oct., 1938, p. 727.

[28] W. H. Auden, *For the Time Being,* p. 130.

[29] W. H. Small, "Early New England Schools," p. 401.

[30] Viz., California, 1863; Ohio, 1857.

[31] C. Whittenburg, "Holiday Observances in the Primary Grades," *Elementary School Journal,* 35:193–204, Nov., 1934.

[32] *Ibid.;* see also *Fact Sheet* issued by the Joint Conference on Religious Holiday Observances in the Public Schools, American Jewish Committee, New York.

[33] *Fact Sheet,* p. 3.

[34] Statement on Religious Observance in the Public Schools Adopted by the Executive Council of the Rabbinical Assembly of America, 1946.

[35] Central Conference of American Rabbis, *Yearbook,* Vol. LV (1945), pp. 89–91.

[36] G. Goldin, "Christmas-Chanukah," *Commentary,* Vol. 10, No. 5, Nov., 1950, p. 417.

[37] *Ibid.,* p. 420.

[38] *Fact Sheet*, pp. 10–11.
[39] *Brother Jonathan*, Dec. 24, 1842, p. 494.
[40] *North American Review*, 84:344 f., April, 1857.
[41] R. R. Doane, *The Measurement of American Wealth*, pp. 42, 43.
[42] *Hartford Courant*, Dec. 27, 1950; Dec. 26, 1949; Dec. 24, 1949.
[43] *Manchester* (N.H.) *Morning Union*, Dec. 26, 1947.
[44] *Hartford Courant*, Dec. 26, 1945.
[45] *Manchester Morning Union*, Dec. 26, 1945.
[46] Letter, Jan. 5, 1948.
[47] M. Tyler, *Family*, Oct., 1939, p. 198.
[48] *New York Times*, Dec. 23, 1950, I:17.
[49] *Ibid.*, Dec. 26, 1913, 2:2.
[50] *Ibid.*, Dec. 26, 1949, 2:4.
[51] *Hartford Courant*, Dec. 22, 1949, p. 1.
[52] *Ibid.*, Dec. 17, 1950.
[53] *New Yorker*, Dec. 23, 1944, p. 11.

Chapter IV. EXPLOITING A FESTIVAL

[1] See *New York Times*, Dec. 23, 1894, 2:6; *New York Daily Tribune*, Dec. 29, 1877, 4:5; Dec. 25, 1888, 4:4; Dec. 28, 1886, 4:3; Dec. 25, 1887, 4:4. See also R. M. Hower, *History of Macy's of New York, 1858–1919*, p. 118.
[2] R. M. Hower, *The History of an Advertising Agency*, pp. 125 f., and *Economic Fluctuations in the United States and the United Kingdom 1918–1922* (League of Nations, Geneva, 1942), p. 13.
[3] This statement is supported by the answers to seven hundred questionnaires returned to the writer shortly after Dec. 25, 1951, and by numerous informal comments and observations.
[4] Stephen Potter, "Christmas-ship," *Atlantic Monthly*, Dec., 1951, p. 35.
[5] See Amos L. Harper, *Bundles for Christmas;* Dorothy Sterling, *The Day After Christmas* and *Good Will Towards Women*.
[6] Letter from Christmas Club headquarters, 230 Park Ave., New York City, dated Dec. 11, 1951, and copy of a press release from the same organization dated Nov. 1, 1951.
[7] Richard B. Gehman, "How to Save Money in Spite of Yourself," *Saturday Evening Post*, Dec. 15, 1951, p. 106.
[8] 1949 Statistical Supplement to the *Survey of Current Busi-*

ness, p. 40; *ibid.,* 1951, p. 40; *Survey of Current Business,* July, 1952, pp. 5–8.

[9] Some preliminary Christmas advertising begins before this date, especially of gift-wrapping materials, but the real emphasis comes after Thanksgiving.

[10] 1949 *Statistical Supplement to Survey of Current Business,* p. 15; *ibid.,* 1951, p. 42; *Survey of Current Business,* July, 1952, pp. 5–8.

[11] *Annual Time Table of Retail Opportunities,* 1951 ed., p. 8.

[12] Thornton B. Moore, "The American Toy Industry's Golden Era," *Business Information Service,* United States Department of Commerce, Aug., 1949.

[13] *Ibid.,* p. 5.

[14] Letter (dated March 19, 1952), from S. Q. Shannon, director of the National Association of Greeting Card Publishers.

[15] Sowder, "Christmas Trees—The Industry," in *Trees—The Yearbook of Agriculture, 1949* (Washington, D.C., United States Government Printing Office), p. 248.

[16] *Ibid.,* p. 249.

[17] 1949 *Statistical Supplement to the Survey of Current Business,* p. 42; *ibid.,* 1951, p. 54; *Survey of Current Business,* Nov., 1952, p. S-11.

[18] 1949 *Statistical Supplement to the Survey of Current Business,* p. 70; *ibid.,* 1951, p. 64; *Business Statistics,* 1953 biennial ed., p. 67.

[19] J. I. Griffin, *Strikes,* pp. 52–55.

[20] "Vacation and Holiday Provisions in Union Agreements, January 1943," Washington, D.C., United States Government Printing Office, 1943, p. 7.

[21] "Christmas Bonuses—1950," *Management Record,* Vol. 13, No. 11, Nov., 1951, pp. 385–387.

[22] See *Labor Relations Reporter,* Vol. 29, No. 11, Dec. 10, 1951, pp. 1075–1078.

[23] Local No. 405, United Automobile, Aircraft and Implement Workers of America, C.I.O.

[24] *Labor Relations Reporter,* Vol. 29, No. 11, Dec. 10, 1951, p. 1077.

[25] Howard P. Abrahams, quoted in "Buyers and Sellers," *New York Herald Tribune,* Sept. 27, 1951, p. 37.

Chapter V. SOCIAL ASPECTS OF CHRISTMAS ART

[1] See May Lamberton Becker's *The Home Book of Christmas,* which contains poems and stories by the writers mentioned.

[2] *Ibid.*

[3] W. H. Auden, *For the Time Being,* p. 130.

[4] *New York Times,* Dec. 11, 1949, X, 9; see also reproduction of Lewandowski's "Three Kings" and Louis Bosa's "Shopping" in *Living for Young Homemakers,* Dec., 1952, pp. 97, 99.

[5] The National Broadcasting Company's television program for this date.

[6] Interesting interpretations of the social causes and character of "popular" art are found in Dwight Macdonald's "A Theory of Popular Culture," *Politics,* Feb., 1944, pp. 20–23, and in Irving Howe's "Notes on Mass Culture," *Politics,* Spring, 1948, pp. 120–123. See also T. S. Eliot, *Notes Towards the Definition of Culture,* Chap. 1.

[7] Another favorite theme in contemporary Christmas plays concerns the last-minute conversion of those who "doubt" or refuse to celebrate Christmas. See A. W. Cook, *Christmas Is a Racket* (Boston, Walter H. Baker Company, 1944).

[8] Interview with Robert L. May, March 11, 1951, in Hartford, Conn.

[9] *Ibid.*

[10] Letter from Robert L. May, Nov. 20, 1951.

[11] Alexander H. Krappe, "Guiding Animals," *American Journal of Folklore,* Vol. 55, No. 218, Oct.–Dec., 1942, pp. 228–246.

[12] Radio dramatic versions have been broadcast on a full hour's program either on the Lux program or on the Screen Directors' Guild at Christmas in 1948, 1949, and 1950: In addition, the motion-picture version of the story has been revived several times since it appeared in June, 1947.

[13] These plays were made available for study through the courtesy of Walter H. Baker Company and Samuel French, Inc. The publishers were asked for plays which were typical of modern Christmas dramas and which were successful commercially. Limitations of space have made it impossible to list the titles in the Bibliography.

[14] Estimate of National Association of Greeting Card Publishers, letter, March 19, 1952.

[15] Reproductions obtained from the Museum of Modern Art, New York, N. Y.

[16] Mr. Sidney Williams, executive secretary of the Chicago Urban League, has kindly provided me with samples of these cards.

[17] The Art Division of the Progressive Citizens of America (New York, N.Y.) produced cards of this type.

[18] See remark quoted by William H. Whyte, Jr., in "The Wives of Management," *Fortune*, Oct., 1951, p. 204.

[19] This is an adaptation of these concepts as developed by David Riesman in *The Lonely Crowd*.

Chapter VI.   THE CULT OF CHRISTMAS

[1] W. D. Love, Jr., *Fast and Thanksgiving Days of New England*. See also J. W. Stedman, "Hartford in 1830: Some Things I Remember About Hartford Sixty Years Ago," *Connecticut Historical Society Bulletin*, Vol. 14, No. 4, Oct., 1949, p. 31.

[2] A. Davis, B. Gardner, and M. Gardner, *Deep South* (Chicago, University of Chicago Press, 1941), p. 449.

[3] However, this includes the return of items purchased throughout the preceding several weeks.

[4] For documentation on one aspect of this topic, see J. Eisenbud, "Negative Reaction to Christmas," *Psychoanalytic Quarterly*, Vol. 10, Oct., 1941, pp. 639–645, and R. Sterba, "On Christmas," *ibid.*, Vol. 13, 1944, pp. 79–83. See also *Mass-observation Bulletin*, "Recipe for Christmas," Christmas, 1948, and results of public-opinion poll on Christmas in *Public Opinion Quarterly*, 14:177–178, Spring, 1950. In addition to unconscious anxieties, there are the very real dangers of loss of life and property at Christmas owing to traffic accidents and fires.

[5] *New York Times* Book Review Section, Oct. 14, 1951, p. 2.

[6] *Hartford Courant*, Dec. 25, 1945, p. A2.

[7] *Life*, Dec. 27, 1948, p. 86. Used by permission.

[8] *Time*, Dec. 25, 1950, p. 28; *New York Times*, Dec. 15, 1952, p. 28; *Hartford Courant*, Nov. 19, 1952, Dec. 18, 1952.

[9] Renzo Sereno, "Some Observations on the Santa Claus Custom," *Psychiatry*, Vol. 14, Nov., 1951, p. 392.

[10] *Hartford Courant*, Dec. 26, 1950; *New Yorker*, Dec. 20, 1952, p. 103.

[11] *Christian Science Monitor*, Magazine Section, Dec. 21, 1946, p. 3.

[12] *New York Times*, Dec. 25, 1937, p. 14 (C).

[13] *Manila Bulletin*, Dec. 20, 1951; *Time*, Jan. 14, 1952, p. 44.

[14] *New York Times*, Jan. 4, 1953, 7:1.

[15] *Ibid.*, Dec. 15, 1952, p. 17; Dec. 24, 1950, 27:6; *Life*, Dec. 17, 1951, p. 32.

[16] *New York Times*, Dec. 23, 1949, 14:3.

[17] *Hartford Courant*, Dec. 5, 1947, p. 10.

[18] *Hartford Courant*, Dec. 25, 1951; *Time*, Jan. 7, 1952, p. 54.

Bibliography

I. Books and Articles on Holidays and Festivals, Especially Christmas

Alofsen, Soloman, MS, "St. Nicholas Festival in Holland," Nov. 21, 1865, New-York Historical Society, New York, N.Y.

Anichtof, Eugene, "St. Nicholas and Artemis," *Folklore*, 5:108–120, June, 1894.

Arthur, Julietta K., "A Century of Christmas Cards," *American Home*, Dec., 1946, pp. 15–18.

Barnett, James H., "Christmas in American Culture," *Psychiatry*, Vol. 9, No. 1, Feb., 1946, pp. 51–65.

———, "The Easter Festival—A Study in Cultural Change," *American Sociological Review*, Vol. 14, No. 1, Feb., 1949, pp. 62–70.

Bauer, Robert C., "Christmas in Old Connecticut," *Connecticut Circle*, Vol. 12, No. 12, Dec., 1949, p. 2.

Brand, John, *Popular Antiquities*, 3 vols. London, Henry G. Bohn, 1848 ed.

Brother Jonathan, editorial comment on Christmas, Dec. 24, 1842, p. 494.

Brown, A. E., "The Ups and Downs of Christmas in New England," *New England Magazine*, 29:479–484, Dec., 1903.

Business Week, "Too Many Santa Clauses," Nov. 20, 1937, p. 40.

Chambers, Robert, ed., *Book of Days: A Miscellany of Popular Antiquities*, 2 vols. Philadelphia, J. B. Lippincott Co., 1914.

Chase, Ernest Dudley, *The Romance of Greeting Cards*. Boston, 1926.

Chrisulis, Mary J., "The Twelve Days: A Study of the Christmas, New Year and Epiphany Holidays Among the Greek People." Unpublished MS, 1949.

Clarke, Ednah Proctor, "The Revolt of Santa Claus," *Ladies' Home Journal*, Dec., 1901, p. 19.

Collier's, "Christmas IS Our Way of Life," 124:78, Dec. 24, 1949.

Collier's Weekly, "What I Think of Santa Claus" (by eighteen authors), Dec. 15, 1923, pp. 10–11.

Cooke, John Esten, "Christmas Time in Old Virginia," *Magazine of American History*, 10:443–459, Dec., 1883.

Crawford, Mary Sinclair, "Life of St. Nicholas," Ph.D. thesis. Philadelphia, University of Pennsylvania, 1923.

Curtis, George William, "Christmas," *Harper's New Monthly Magazine*, 68:3–16, Dec., 1883.

Davidson, Frida, "How Our Christmas Customs Came," *Natural History*, Vol. 27, No. 6, Nov. 11, 1928, pp. 617–625.

Department of Commerce, *Special Days, Weeks and Months in 1951*. Washington, United States Government Printing Office, 1950.

Douglas, George W., *American Book of Days*. New York, H. W. Wilson Co., 1937.

Eisenbud, Jule, "Negative Reactions to Christmas," *Psychoanalytic Quarterly*, Vol. 10, No. 4, Oct., 1941, pp. 639–645.

Fehrle, Eugen, *Deutsche Feste und Volksbräuche*. 2nd ed., Leipzig, 1927.

Feilberg, H. F., Jul, 2 vols. (in Danish). Copenhagen, The Schubotheske Press, 1904.

Fortune, "Memo: To All Personnel. Subject: Xmas Party," Dec., 1950, pp. 91–93.

———, "Standard Santas," Dec., 1937, p. 12.

———, "Christmas Business," Dec., 1951, pp. 103–106.

Fowler, Warde W., *The Roman Festivals of the Period of the Republic*. London, Macmillan and Co., Ltd., 1899.

Freemantle, A., "Christmas in Literature," *Commonweal*, 43:185–188, Dec. 7, 1945.

Furman, Gabriel, "Diary" (contains scattered comments on the observance of Christmas in the United States about 1845), *New-York Historical Society*, New York, N.Y.

Glenn, Mary Willcox, "The Santa Claus Letters—A Departure in Post Office Regulations," *Charities and the Commons*, 21:384–388, Dec. 5, 1908.

Goldin, Grace, "Christmas-Chanukah—December Is the Cruelest Month," *Commentary*, Vol. 10, No. 5, Nov., 1950, pp. 416–425.

de Groot, Adrianus, *Sint Nicolaas, Patroon van Liefde*. Amsterdam, 1949.

Hale, Edward E., "Christmas in Boston," *New England Magazine*, Vol. 1, No. 4, Dec., 1889, pp. 355–367.

Hamilton, Mary, *Greek Saints and Their Festivals*. Edinburgh and London, William Blackwood and Sons, 1910.

Hare, Kate, "Christmas Folklore" (a bibliography), *Quarterly Review*, Jan., 1935, pp. 31–46.

Harrison, Michael, *The Story of Christmas*. London, Odhams Press, Ltd., 1951.

Hatcher, John H., *"Ex parte Santa Claus"* (an unjudicial opinion), *The Syllabus Service*, Vol. 6, Dec. 23, 1927. Charleston, W. Va. (publisher, Mrs. G. C. Goff).

Hazeltine, Mary Emogene, *Anniversaries and Holidays*. Chicago, American Library Association, 1944.

Heilbron, Bertha L., "Christmas and New Year's on the Frontier," *Minnesota History*, Vol. 16, No. 4, Dec., 1935, pp. 373–390.

Johnston, Leslie Dent, "Classical Origins of Christmas Customs," Ph.D. thesis. University of Illinois, 1936.

Joint Conference on Religious Holiday Observances in the Public Schools, 1949: *Fact Sheet—Background Information and Bibliography*. Issued by the Synagogue Council of America and the National Community Relations Advisory Council, New York, N.Y.

Jones, Charles W., "Knickerbocker Santa Claus," *New-York Historical Society Quarterly* (in press, 1954).

Kellner, K. A. Heinrich, *Heortology: A History of the Christian Festivals from Their Origin to the Present Day*. London, Kegan Paul, Trench, Trubner & Co., 1908.

Klinefelter, Walter, *A Bibliographical Check List of Christmas Books*. Portland, 1937.

Kluckhohn, Clyde, "Myths and Rituals: A General Theory," *Harvard Theological Review*, Vol. 35, No. 1, Jan., 1942, pp. 45–79.

La Joie, Ray A., "Christmas Art Is Going Highbrow," *Connecticut Circle*, Vol. 13, No. 12, Dec., 1950, p. 5.

Lamb, Martha J., "Christmas Season in Dutch New York," *Magazine of American History*, 10:471–474, Dec., 1883.

Lee, F. W., "Christmas in Virginia Before the War," *Southern Workman*, 37:686–689, 1908.

Lehman, E., "Christmas Customs," in Hastings' *Encyclopaedia of Religion and Ethics*, 3:608–610.

Lewy, Immanuel, "A Christmas Letter by a Jew," *Reconstructionist*, Vol. 14, No. 17, Dec. 24, 1948, pp. 18–20.

Life, "Christmas at Home," Dec. 24, 1945, pp. 15 f.

———, "Christmas at Macy's," Dec. 13, 1948, pp. 91–94.

———, "From Santa Claus to Santa Stooge," Dec. 17, 1951, pp. 32–33.

———, "Life Goes to an Office Christmas Party," Dec. 27, 1948, pp. 86–87.

———, "Miracle on 34th Street," June 16, 1947, pp. 65–68.

Literary Digest, "Pagan Christmas Cards," 112:24, Jan. 30, 1924.

———, "Santa Claus Shop in New York," 51:1497–1498, Dec. 25, 1915.

Love, W. De Loss, Jr., *Fast and Thanksgiving Days of New England*. Boston, Houghton Mifflin Co., 1895.

McCurdy, Robert M., and Edith M. Coulter, *A Bibliography of Articles Relating to Holidays*. Boston, Boston Book Co., 1907.

McKnight, George H., *St. Nicholas*. New York, G. P. Putnam's Sons, 1917.

McWhorter, G. C., "The Holidays," *Harper's New Monthly Magazine*, 32:164–172, Dec., 1865.

Management Record, "Christmas Bonuses—1950," Vol. 13, No. 11, Nov., 1951, pp. 385–387.

Manila Bulletin, Christmas ed. Philippine Islands, Dec. 20, 1951.

Manning, Maybelle, "You Can't Tell Some People There Is No Santa Claus," *American Home*, Dec., 1946, p. 25.

Marchant, Annie d'Armond, "Christmas in Brazil," *Bulletin, Pan-American Union*, Dec., 1936. Washington, United States Government Printing Office.

Mass-observation, "Notes on Christmas," London, 1951.

———, Reports on Christmas Observance in England in 1940, 1941 (typescript), London (n.d.).

Meissen, Karl, "Nikolauskult und Nikolausbrauch im Abendlande, Heft 9–12, *Forschungen zur Volkskunde*, Düsseldorf, 1931.

Miles, Clement A., *Christmas in Ritual and Tradition*. London, T. Fisher Unwin, 1912.

Monks, James L., *Great Catholic Festivals*. New York, Henry Schuman, Inc., 1951.

Munch, Peter Andreas, *Norse Mythology*. London, Oxford University Press, 1926.

Nation, "An International Saint," 109:789, Dec. 20, 1919.

Nelson, A. N., Private communication on celebration of Christmas in the Philippine Islands, Feb. 24, 1952.

Nelson, Edna Du Pree, "Santa Claus and His American Debut," *American Collector*, Dec., 1939, p. 8–9.

Neuhoff, Dorothy A., "Christmas in Colonial America," *Social Studies*, Vol. XL, No. 8, Dec., 1949, pp. 339–349.

New Mirror, "Knickerbockers and Leather Breeches," Vol. II, No. 13, Dec. 30, 1843, pp. 193–194.

New Yorker, "St. Monty," 18:16–17, Dec. 19, 1942.

Nitzsche, G. E., "The Christmas Putz of the Pennsylvania Germans," *Publications of the Pennsylvania German Folklore Society*, Vol. 6, No. 1, 1941, pp. 1–28.

North American Review, "Holidays," 84:334–363, April, 1857.

O'Neil, C. C., "Christmas Customs and Legends," *Catholic World*, 124:289–296, Dec., 1924.

Outlook, "Immortal Santa Claus," 112:66, Jan. 12, 1916.

Pastoral Psychology, Vol. 2, No. 19, Dec., 1951. (Entire issue devoted to Christmas.)

Pollock, Channing, "I Ran Away from Christmas," in *Guideposts in Chaos*. New York, Thomas Y. Crowell Co., 1942.

———, "There's Got to Be a Santa Claus," *Rotarian*, Dec., 1941, p. 7.

Potter, Stephen, "Christmas-ship, or The Art of Giving and Receiving," *Atlantic Monthly*, Dec., 1951, pp. 35–36.

Richards, Katherine Lambert, *How Christmas Came to the Sunday-Schools*. New York, Dodd, Mead & Co., 1934.

Rietschel, George, *Weihnachten in Kirche, Kunst und Volksleben*. Leipzig, 1902.

Riis, Jacob, "Merry Christmas in the Tenements," *Century Magazine*, Vol. 55, No. 2, Dec., 1897, pp. 163–182.

Rodgers, Edith Cooperrider, *Discussion of Holidays in the Later Middle Ages*. New York, Columbia University Press, 1940.

Rominger, Charles H., "Christmas in Bethlehem in Pennsylvania," *New England Magazine*, Vol. 45, No. 4, Dec., 1911, pp. 421–426.

Saturday Review, "American Holidays," 62:18–19, July 3, 1886.

Segal, Abraham, "Christmas in the Public Schools—The Problem," *Reconstructionist*, Vol. 14, No. 16, Dec. 10, 1948, pp. 17–22.

Sereno, Renzo, "Some Observations on the Santa Claus Custom," *Psychiatry*, Vol. 14, No. 4, Nov., 1951, pp. 387–396.

Shaw, S. Adele, "The Americanization of Christmas," *New Republic*, 33:171, Jan. 10, 1923.

Sowder, Arthur M., "Christmas Trees—The Tradition," *Trees —The Yearbook of Agriculture, 1949*, Washington, United States Government Printing Office.

Spencer, O. M., "Christmas Throughout Christendom," *Harper's New Monthly Magazine*, 46:241–257, Dec., 1872.

Sterba, Richard, "On Christmas," *Psychoanalytic Quarterly*, 13:79–83, 1944.

Sweet, William Warren, "Christmas in American History," *Chicago Theological Seminary Register*, 22:12–14, Nov., 1932.

Tille, Alexander, "German Christmas and the Christmas Tree," *Folklore*, 3:166–182, June, 1892.

———, *Yule and Christmas*. London, David Nutt, 1899.

Tittle, Walter, *Colonial Holidays*. New York, Doubleday, Page & Co., 1910.

Tyler, Martha, "Christmas Giving and Casework Planning," *Family*, Oct., 1939, pp. 198–200.

United States Department of Labor, *Vacation and Holiday Provisions in Union Agreements*. Washington, United States Government Printing Office, 1943.

Urlin, Ethel L., *Festivals, Holy Days, and Saints' Days*. London, Simpkin, Marshall, Hamilton, Kent & Co., Ltd., 1915.

Usener, Herman, *Das Weihnachtsfest*. Bonn, 1889 ed.

Vail, R. W. G., "Santa Claus Visits the Hudson," *New-York Historical Society Quarterly*, Vol. 35, No. 4, Oct., 1951, pp. 337–343.

Van De Graft, C. Catherine, "Sinterklaas, Goedheilig Man," *Haagsch Maandblad*, Vol. 8, No. 12, Dec., 1927, pp. 626–636.

De Voto, Bernard, "Seed Corn and Mistletoe," *Harper's Magazine*, 174:109–112, Dec., 1936.

Walker, Norman M., "The Holidays in Early Louisiana," *Magazine of American History*, Vol. 10, Dec., 1883, pp. 460–466.

Wall, Alexander J., Jr., "St. Nicholas at the Society," *New-York Historical Society Quarterly Bulletin*, Vol. 25, No. 1, Jan., 1941, pp. 10–16.

Wallis, Wilson D., *Culture and Progress*, pp. 117–122. New York, McGraw-Hill Book Co., Inc., 1930.

Walsh, W. T., "Connecticut Christmas," *Catholic World*, 130:302–306, Dec. 21, 1930.

Walsh, William S., *Curiosities of Popular Customs*. Philadelphia, J. B. Lippincott Co., 1897.

Watt, W. W., "Christmas, 1943—A Dickens Centenary," *Saturday Review of Literature*, 26:16–18, Dec. 4, 1943.

Weaver, Phil, Jr., "Christmas and Christmases," *Overland Monthly*, Series 2, Vol. 21, Jan., 1893, pp. 32–44.

Webb, Walter Prescott, "Christmas and New Year in Texas," *Southwestern Historical Quarterly* 44:357–379, July, 1940–April, 1941.

West, Henry Litchfield, "Who Wrote ' 'Twas the Night Before Christmas'?" *The Bookman*, 52:300–305, Dec., 1920.

White, Gleeson, "Christmas Cards—Their Chief Designs," *Studio*, Dec. 25, 1894.

Whiteside, Stanley, "I Feel Like a Heel, Playing Santa," *Saturday Evening Post*, Dec. 16, 1950, p. 25.

Whittenburg, Clarice, "Holiday Observance in the Primary Grades," *Elementary School Journal*, 35:193–204, Nov., 1934.

Wilson, Edmund, "Dickens—The Two Scrooges," in *The Wound and the Bow*. Boston, Houghton Mifflin Co., 1941.

Witt, Louis, "The Jews Celebrate Christmas," *Christian Century*, 56:1497–1498, Dec. 6, 1939.

Wright, Sylvia, "Get Away from Me with Those Christmas Gifts," *Harper's Magazine*, Vol. 205, No. 1231, Dec., 1952, pp. 29–32.

II. *"Christmas" Literature*

Auden, W. H., *For the Time Being*. New York, Random House, 1944.

Becker, May Lamberton, ed., *The Home Book of Christmas*. New York, Dodd, Mead & Co., 1941.

Cummings, E. E., *Santa Claus: A Morality*. New York, Henry Holt & Co., 1946.

Davies, Valentine, *Miracle on 34th Street*. New York, Harcourt, Brace & Co., 1947.

Dickens, Charles, *A Christmas Carol*. New York, Penguin Books, Inc., 1946 ed.

Eddy, Mary Baker, *What Christmas Means to Me, and Other Christmas Messages*. Boston (published by the trustees under the will of Mary Baker G. Eddy), 1949.

Moore, Clement C., "A Visit from St. Nicholas." New York, Henry M. Onderdonk, 1848 ed.

III. *Miscellaneous*

Bossard, James H. S., and Eleanor S. Boll, *Ritual in Family Living*. Philadelphia, University of Pennsylvania Press, 1950.

Brewer, William Henry, *Up and Down California in 1860–1864*. New Haven, Yale University Press, 1930.

Broun, Heywood, "It Seems to Heywood Broun," *Nation*, 125: 728, Dec. 28, 1927.

Bureau of Advertising, "Annual Time Table of Retail Opportunities, 1951 Edition," New York: American Newspaper Publishers Association, Inc.

Chase, Ernest Dudley, *The Greeting Card Industry*. Boston, Bellman Publishing Co., Inc., 1946.

Davis, Allison, and Burleigh Gardner and Mary Gardner, *Deep South*. Chicago, University of Chicago Press, 1941.

Doane, Robert R., *The Measurement of American Wealth*. New York, Harper & Brothers, 1933.

Duchesne, L., *Christian Worship—Its Origin and Evolution*. New York, The Macmillan Company, 1931 ed.

Fichter, Joseph H., *Southern Parish: The Dynamics of a City Church*. Chicago, University of Chicago Press, 1951.

Fish, Carl R., *The Rise of the Common Man, 1830–1850*. New York, The Macmillan Company, 1927.

Geiger, Paul, und Richard Weiss, *Atlas der Schweizerischen Volkskunde*. Basel, Schweizerische Gesellschaft für Volkskunde, 1950.

Gesell, Arnold, "Human Infancy and the Ontogenesis of Behavior," *American Scientist*, 37:529–553, 1949.

Griffin, John I., *Strikes*. New York, Columbia University Press, 1939.

Henry, William E., "A Study of the Application of Socio-Psychological Research to the Problems of Business and Industry," *Journal of Social Psychology*, 27:37–61, 1948.

Homans, George C., "Anxiety and Ritual," *American Anthropologist*, Vol. 43, No. 2, Pt. 1, April–June, 1941, pp. 164–172.

Hough, P. M., *Dutch Life in Town and Country*. New York, G. P. Putnam's Sons, 1901.

Howe, Irving, "Notes on Mass Culture," *Politics*, Spring, 1948, pp. 120–123.

Hower, Ralph M., *The History of an Advertising Agency*

. . . (rev. ed.). Cambridge, Harvard University Press, 1949.

——, *History of Macy's of New York, 1858–1919.* Cambridge, Harvard University Press, 1943.

Irving, Washington, *Knickerbocker's History of New York.* New York, G. P. Putnam's Sons, 1894 ed.

Jackson, T. A., *Charles Dickens: The Progress of a Radical.* New York, International Publishers, 1938.

Johnson, Guion Griffis, *Ante-Bellum North Carolina.* Chapel Hill, University of North Carolina Press, 1937.

Johnston, Leslie Dent, "The Lares and the Kalends Log," *Classical Philology,* 34:342–356, Oct., 1939.

Kiefer, Monica, *American Children Through Their Books, 1700–1835.* Philadelphia, University of Pennsylvania Press, 1948.

Klees, Fredric, *The Pennsylvania Dutch.* New York, The Macmillan Company, 1951.

Krappe, Alexander H., "Guiding Animals," *Journal of American Folklore,* Vol. 55, No. 218, Oct.–Dec., 1942, pp. 228–246.

Lowenthal, Leo, "Historical Perspectives of Popular Culture," *American Journal of Sociology,* Vol. LV, No. 4, Jan., 1950, pp. 323–332.

Macdonald, Dwight, "A Theory of 'Popular Culture,' " *Politics,* Feb., 1944, pp. 20–23.

Manross, William Wilson, *The Episcopal Church in the United States, 1800–1840.* New York, Columbia University Press, 1938.

Mather, Cotton, "The Diary of Cotton Mather, Part II," *Massachusetts Historical Collections,* Vol. VIII.

Maurois, André, *Dickens.* London, John Lane, 1934.

Nevins, Allan, *The Emergence of Modern America, 1865–1878.* New York, The Macmillan Company, 1927.

Paine, Albert Bigelow, *Thomas Nast, His Period and His Pictures.* New York, The Macmillan Company, 1904.

Panofsky, Erwin, *Studies in Iconology; Humanistic Themes in the Art of the Renaissance.* New York, Oxford University Press, 1939.

Pierce, Carl Horton, *New Harlem Past and Present.* New York, New Harlem Publishing Co., 1903.

Reynolds, H. W., "Editorial Notes on the Writings of Henry W. Livingston, Jr.," *Dutchess County Historical Society Yearbook,* 27:85–104, 1942.

Riesman, David, *The Lonely Crowd.* New Haven, Yale University Press, 1950.

Stroup, Herbert Hewitt, *The Jehovah's Witnesses*. New York, Columbia University Press, 1945.

Sussman, Marvin, "Family Continuity: A Study of Factors Which Affect Relationships Between Families at Generational Levels," Ph.D. thesis. Yale, 1951 (typescript).

Thomas, John L., "Religious Training in the Roman Catholic Family," *American Journal of Sociology*, Vol. LVII, No. 2, Sept., 1951, pp. 178–183.

United States Department of Agriculture, *Trees—The Yearbook of Agriculture, 1949*. Washington, United States Government Printing Office.

United States Department of Commerce, *The American Toy Industry's Golden Era*. Washington, United States Government Printing Office, 1949.

Whyte, William H., Jr., "The Wives of Management," *Fortune*, Oct., 1951, pp. 86–213.

Wright, J. E., and D. S. Corbett, *Pioneer Life in Western Pennsylvania*. Pittsburgh, University of Pittsburgh Press, 1940.

Yearbook, Central Conference of American Rabbis, Vol. LV, 1945.

Index